1st EDITION

Perspectives on Diseases and Disorders

Tourette Syndrome

Mary E. Williams
Book Editor

Detroit • New York • San Francisco • New Haven, Conn • Waterville, Maine • London

Elizabeth Des Chenes, *Director, Publishing Solutions*

For more information, contact:
Greenhaven Press
27500 Drake Rd.
Farmington Hills, MI 48331-3535
Or you can visit our Internet site at gale.cengage.com

For product information and technology assistance, contact us at

Gale Customer Support, 1-800-877-4253
For permission to use material from this text or product, submit all requests online at www.cengage.com/permissions

Further permissions questions can be e-mailed to permissionrequest@cengage.com

Articles in Greenhaven Press anthologies are often edited for length to meet page requirements. In addition, original titles of these works are changed to clearly present the main thesis and to explicitly indicate the author's opinion. Every effort is made to ensure that Greenhaven Press accurately reflects the original intent of the authors. Every effort has been made to trace the owners of copyrighted material.

Cover image © Sebastian Knight/ShutterStock.com

LIBRARY OF CONGRESS CATALOGING-IN-PUBLICATION DATA

Tourette syndrome / Mary E. Williams, book editor.
    p. cm. -- (Perspectives on diseases and disorders)
  Includes bibliographical references and index.
  ISBN 978-0-7377-6360-7 (hardcover)
  1. Tourette syndrome--Juvenile literature. I. Williams, Mary E., 1960-
RC375.T67 2012
616.8'3--dc23

2012023737

Printed in the United States of America
1 2 3 4 5 6 7 16 15 14 13 12

CONTENTS

FOREWORD

"Medicine, to produce health, has to examine disease."
—Plutarch

Independent research on a health issue is often the first step to complement discussions with a physician. But locating accurate, well-organized, understandable medical information can be a challenge. A simple Internet search on terms such as "cancer" or "diabetes," for example, returns an intimidating number of results. Sifting through the results can be daunting, particularly when some of the information is inconsistent or even contradictory. The Greenhaven Press series Perspectives on Diseases and Disorders offers a solution to the often overwhelming nature of researching diseases and disorders.

From the clinical to the personal, titles in the Perspectives on Diseases and Disorders series provide students and other researchers with authoritative, accessible information in unique anthologies that include basic information about the disease or disorder, controversial aspects of diagnosis and treatment, and first-person accounts of those impacted by the disease. The result is a well-rounded combination of primary and secondary sources that, together, provide the reader with a better understanding of the disease or disorder.

Each volume in Perspectives on Diseases and Disorders explores a particular disease or disorder in detail. Material for each volume is carefully selected from a wide range of sources, including encyclopedias, journals, newspapers, nonfiction books, speeches, government documents, pamphlets, organization newsletters, and position papers. Articles in the first chapter provide an authoritative, up-to-date overview that covers symptoms, causes and effects, treatments, cures, and medical advances. The second chapter presents a substantial number of opposing viewpoints on controversial treatments and other current debates relating to the volume topic. The third chapter offers a variety of personal perspectives on the disease or disorder. Patients, doctors, caregivers, and loved ones represent just some of the voices found in this narrative chapter.

Each Perspectives on Diseases and Disorders volume also includes:

- An **annotated table of contents** that provides a brief summary of each article in the volume.
- An **introduction** specific to the volume topic.
- Full-color **charts and graphs** to illustrate key points, concepts, and theories.
- Full-color **photos** that show aspects of the disease or disorder and enhance textual material.
- **"Fast Facts"** that highlight pertinent additional statistics and surprising points.
- A **glossary** providing users with definitions of important terms.
- A **chronology** of important dates relating to the disease or disorder.
- An annotated list of **organizations to contact** for students and other readers seeking additional information.
- A **bibliography** of additional books and periodicals for further research.
- A detailed **subject index** that allows readers to quickly find the information they need.

Whether a student researching a disorder, a patient recently diagnosed with a disease, or an individual who simply wants to learn more about a particular disease or disorder, a reader who turns to Perspectives on Diseases and Disorders will find a wealth of information in each volume that offers not only basic information, but also vigorous debate from multiple perspectives.

INTRODUCTION

For all of his life, twelve-year-old Jaylen Arnold of Lakeland, Florida, has lived with several challenging disorders: Asperger's syndrome, an autism spectrum disorder characterized by difficulties in social interaction; obsessive-compulsive disorder (OCD), a condition in which one becomes trapped in a pattern of repetitive thoughts and behaviors; and Tourette syndrome (TS), a neurological disorder characterized by repeated, involuntary movements and sounds known as tics. TS is perhaps Jaylen's most publicly noticeable condition—his tics can include sharp barking noises, gurgling sounds, sudden head twitches, and flailing arms. As is true for many TS patients, Jaylen's symptoms go through waxing and waning cycles—periods of an increase in the number and severity of tics followed by periods of fewer, less severe tics.

In 2009, when Jaylen was nine years old, his tics got worse when he started attending a new school. Classmates bullied him by mimicking his involuntary movements, and the distress this caused only led to an increase in the amount and severity of his tics. Some students directly rejected him, saying, "You're a weird kid. You should just go back to where you came from."[1] In a television interview, Jaylen recalls, "That made me feel really sad—*real* sad."[2] School was not the only place where Jaylen faced rejection and misunderstanding. Karen Arnold, Jaylen's mother, recounts a frequent reaction when she is out with her son in public: "People say out loud, where we can hear them, 'Ooh, what's wrong with that child? He has a demon in him.'"[3]

Demonic possession was, in fact, the common explanation for TS in earlier eras. But progress in science

PERSPECTIVES ON DISEASES AND DISORDERS

during the eighteenth and nineteenth centuries brought new understandings to the forefront, particularly in 1885, when French physician Georges Albert Édouard Brutus Gilles de la Tourette published *Study of a Nervous Affliction*, an account of nine patients who suffered from various tics. He concluded that their patterns of involuntary sounds and movement sprang from one particular medical condition—the syndrome that now bears his name. Developments in the late twentieth century led to the recognition that TS is an inherited neurological disorder—and not a psychological disturbance, as many scientists had previously theorized. Today experts contend that up to 7 percent of youths in special education and 3 percent of children in regular education classrooms—three out of one thousand—have TS. Many have never been diagnosed—due in part to the fact that some people with TS have mild, barely noticeable symptoms. Another reason for underdiagnosis, however, is a lingering lack of awareness about the disorder among the general public and in educational settings.

Jaylen Arnold has decided to confront this lack of awareness. Incorporating blogs and videos, he created a website, Jaylens Challenge, to change the perception of kids with TS and its related disorders, including OCD. Much of the focus of his challenge is on bullying. As Jaylen explains, "I wanted to find a way to help kids that were still getting bullied. When I was copied and laughed at for my tics, it made my TS much worse because it stressed me. . . . When I went back to the school that made fun of me and told them about my problems, the kids listened and said they were sorry. So I thought, 'this is easy, someone just needs to tell all these bad kids.'"[4]

Adults, including parents and teachers, also need to be educated about the issue of TS and bullying. As Kathy Giordano, an education specialist for the Tourette Syndrome Association, points out:

People do not understand TS or the related difficulties that often are associated with TS. . . . Students and even professionals often believe that the child is saying or acting in a manner that is purposeful. Schools often do not know how to respond to teasing and bullying because they believe that the child is doing these things on purpose to get attention. Everyone knows that a student is not purposefully using a wheel chair because they think it is funny or want to be disrespectful. Symptoms of TS are significantly misinterpreted and therefore school personnel do not know how to respond.[5]

Giordano suggests two strategies for changing an educational environment that enables harassment and bullying: educating people and fostering the strengths of the student with TS. When teachers, classmates, and school personnel learn the facts about the disorder, understand-

Children with Tourette syndrome are often the victims of bullying. (© Bubbles Photolibrary/ Alamy)

ing and acceptance are likely to emerge. Likewise, when students with TS receive encouragement for what they are able to do well, their chances to flourish academically and socially are greatly improved.

Megan Moiser, a bullying prevention trainer who has TS, offers additional guidelines for students dealing with bullying. Most importantly, a child should never ignore bullying; doing so is a blanket acceptance of peer abuse. The child should instead find an adult at the school that he or she trusts to talk with in confidence about the bullying—a way of identifying the problem that does not require becoming a "tattletale." Moiser does not encourage physically fighting back, because such responses can easily backfire: "Often . . . [when] the youngster with TS stands up to the bully, [he or she] gets suspended from school and labeled as an aggressive and dangerous person."[6] While violence is not a good confrontational strategy, calm assertiveness is: "Practice standing up straight, making eye contact and saying 'Stop it. You can't do that to me,'"[7] Moiser says. At that point, the student should quietly walk away and seek out a group of peers or a trusted adult.

Jaylen's anti-bullying campaign has blossomed to include speeches and appearances at various schools as well as television interviews and public service announcements. At one question-and-answer session, a student asked Jaylen, "Do you get picked on anymore?" Jaylen answered, "No, because all my friends defended me."[8] On a similar note, Jaylen's mother hopes for a day when increased public awareness about TS will dispel misunderstanding and superstition: "When I walk into a grocery store, I want someone to be able to look at my child and say, 'Wow, that little boy has Tourette syndrome.'"[9]

The publishers of *Perspectives on Diseases and Disorders: Tourette Syndrome* also aim to counteract myths and misperceptions about this widely misunderstood condition. In this volume, physicians, specialists, educators, and journalists—as well as TS patients themselves—discuss the challenges of living with and treating a neurological disorder that greatly impacts the lives of thousands of people each day.

Notes

1. Quoted in Katie Couric and Kelly Cobiella, "The American Spirit (Jaylen Arnold)," *CBS Evening News*, November 4, 2009.
2. Quoted in Couric and Cobiella, "The American Spirit (Jaylen Arnold)."
3. Quoted in Jeremy Campbell, "Anti-Bullying Message from 10-Year-Old Lakeland Boy," Fox 13 News (Tampa Bay, FL), September 12, 2010. www.myfoxtampabay .com/dpp/news/local/polk/anti-bullying-09-12-2010.
4. Quoted in Tourette Syndrome Association, "Bullying 101: What Children, Parents, and Teachers Need to Know," *Inside TSA*, Spring 2010.
5. Quoted in Tourette Syndrome Association, "Bullying 101."
6. Quoted in Tourette Syndrome Association, "Bullying 101."
7. Quoted in Tourette Syndrome Association, "Bullying 101."
8. Quoted in Couric and Cobiella, "The American Spirit (Jaylen Arnold)."
9. Quoted in Jeremy Campbell, "Anti-Bullying Message from 10-Year-Old Lakeland Boy."

CHAPTER 1

Understanding Tourette Syndrome

Tourette Syndrome: An Overview

Belinda Rowland and Rebecca J. Frey

In the following selection medical writers Belinda Rowland and Rebecca J. Frey provide a general description of Tourette syndrome (TS), noting its major features, symptoms, causes, and strategies for treatment. TS is an inherited neurological disorder characterized by repetitive, spasmodic, unintentional muscle movements and vocalizations known as tics. The symptoms of TS range from very mild to dramatic—some people with TS have symptoms that are barely noticeable, while others may have tics so severe that they cannot perform simple activities. While only a minority of TS patients have a tic known as coprolalia, in which one involuntarily utters obscenities, a significant percentage of people with TS have co-occurring conditions such as dyslexia, obsessive-compulsive behaviors, or attention-deficit/hyperactivity disorder. There is no cure for TS, but a variety of treatments and therapies may reduce the severity and frequency of tics. Many patients find that their tics become milder as they grow older; others find ways to live with their disorder. Those who suffer from the most severe tics, however, have more profound challenges with social development and mental health.

Photo on previous page. Tourette syndrome causes "tics," or involuntary movements or vocalizations. (© Paul Bock/Alamy)

SOURCE: Belinda Rowland and Rebecca J. Frey, "Tourette Syndrome," *Gale Encyclopedia of Alternative Medicine* 3E, v. 3, Copyright © 2009 Cengage Learning, pp. 2247–2250. All rights reserved. Reproduced by permission.

Tourette syndrome (TS) is an inherited disease of the nervous system, first described more than a century ago by a pioneering French neurologist, George Gilles de la Tourette. Before they are 18 years of age, patients with TS develop motor tics; that is, repeated, jerky, purposeless muscle movements in almost any part of the body. Patients also develop vocal tics, which occur in the form of loud grunting or barking noises, or in some cases words or phrases. In most patients, the tics come and go, and are often replaced by different sounds or movements. The tics may become more complex as the patient grows older.

Characteristics of Tourette Syndrome

TS is three times more common in men than in women. The motor tics, which usually occur in brief episodes several times a day, may make it very hard for the patient to perform such simple acts as tying shoelaces, not to mention work-related tasks or driving. In addition, TS may have negative effects on the patient's social development. Some patients have an irresistible urge to curse or use offensive racial terms (a condition called coprolalia), although these impulses are not under voluntary control. Other people may not enjoy associating with TS patients. Even if they are accepted socially, TS patients live in fear of offending others and embarrassing themselves. In time, they may close themselves off from former friends and even relatives.

It is important to note, however, that the symptoms of Tourette syndrome are not always dramatic and are often overlooked in people with mild cases of the disorder. A 2001 report published in *Pain & Central Nervous System Week*, in fact, states that TS is much more common than doctors had thought. A study of 1,596 special-education children in Rochester, NY, found that 8% met the criteria for TS, and 27% had a tic disorder. In Rochester's general population, 3% were found to have Tourette syndrome,

Some Tourette patients have coprolalia, an irresistible urge to curse or use offensive racial epithets. (© Paul Brown/Photo Researchers, Inc.)

and 20% had a tic disorder. The rate of 3% in the general population is 50–75 times higher than the usual estimates given.

The tics of TS are often described as involuntary, meaning that patients cannot stop them. This description is not strictly true, however. A tic is a very strong urge to make a certain motion or sound. It is more like an itch that demands to be scratched. Some patients are able to control their tics for several hours, but once they are allowed expression, they are even stronger and last longer. Tics become worse when the patient is under stress, and usually are much less of a problem during sleep.

Some people with TS have trouble paying attention. They often seem grumpy and may have periods of depression. TS patients may think the same thoughts over and over, a mental tic known as an obsession. It is these features that place TS patients on the border between diseases of the nervous system and psychiatric illness. In fact, before research showed that the brains of TS patients undergo abnormal chemical changes, many doctors were convinced that TS was a mental disorder. It still is not clear whether these behaviors are a direct result of TS itself, or a reaction to the stress of having to live with the disease.

What Causes Tourette Syndrome?

Tourette syndrome has been linked to parts of the brain known as the basal ganglia, which regulate movements and [are] involved in concentration, paying attention, and decision-making. Research has also demonstrated that in TS, there is a malfunction in the brain's production or use of important substances called neurotransmitters. Neurotransmitters are chemicals that control the signals that are sent along the nerve cells. The neurotransmitters dopamine and serotonin have been implicated in TS; noradrenaline is thought to be the most important stimulant. Medications that mimic noradrenaline may cause tics in susceptible patients.

> **FAST FACT**
>
> A genetic predisposition to TS may express itself as a milder tic disorder or obsessive-compulsive behaviors rather than full-blown TS, notes the National Institute of Neurological Disorders and Stroke.

TS has a genetic component. If one parent has TS, each child has a 50% chance of getting the abnormal gene. Seven of every 10 girls who inherit the gene, and nearly all boys who inherit it, will develop symptoms of TS. Overall, about one in every 2,500 persons has full-blown TS. Three times as many will have some features, usually chronic motor tics or obsessive thoughts. Patients with TS are more likely to have trouble controlling their impulses, to have dyslexia or other learning problems, and to talk in their sleep or wake frequently. Compulsive behavior, such as constantly washing the hands or repeatedly checking that a door is locked, is a common feature of TS. Compulsions are seen in 30–90% of all TS patients.

Recent research findings suggest that Tourette syndrome may also be related to an autoimmune response. A subset of TS patients have symptoms triggered by infection with Group A beta-hemolytic streptococci. In addition, blood serum antibodies against human basal ganglia have been found in patients with TS.

Symptoms

Motor tics in TS can be classified as simple or complex. Simple tics are sudden, brief movements involving a single group of muscles or a few groups, which may be repeated several times. Complex tics consist of a repeated pattern

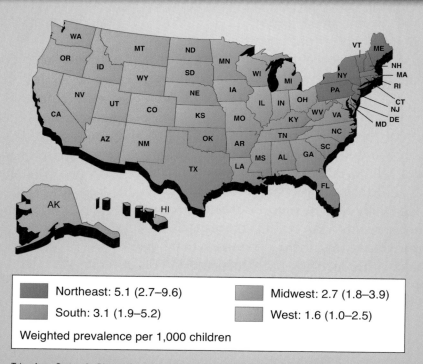

Prevalence of Diagnosed Tourette Syndrome in Children 6–17 Years of Age, by Region

Northeast: 5.1 (2.7–9.6)

Midwest: 2.7 (1.8–3.9)

South: 3.1 (1.9–5.2)

West: 1.6 (1.0–2.5)

Weighted prevalence per 1,000 children

Taken from: Centers for Disease Control and Prevention, November 7, 2011. www.cdc.gov.

of movements that can involve several muscle groups and usually occur in the same order. For instance, a boy with TS may repeatedly move his head from side to side, blink his eyes, open his mouth, and stretch his neck. Vocal tics may be sounds or noises that lack all meaning, or repeated words and phrases that can be understood. Tics tend to get worse and better in cycles, and patients can develop new tics as they grow older. The symptoms of TS may get much better for weeks or months at a time, only to worsen later.

Types of Tics

The following examples show why TS can be such a strange and dramatic disorder:

- Simple motor tics. These may include blinking the eyes, pouting the lips, shaking or jerking the head, shrugging the shoulders, and grimacing or making faces. Any part of the body may be tensed up or rapidly jerked, or a patient may suddenly kick. Rapid finger movements are common, as are snapping the jaws and clicking the teeth.
- Complex motor tics. These may include jumping, touching parts of the body or certain objects, smelling things over and over, stamping the feet, and twirling about. Some TS patients throw objects, others arrange things in a certain way. Biting, head-banging, writhing movements, rolling the eyes up or from side to side, and sticking out the tongue may all be seen. A child may write the same letter or word over and over, or may tear apart papers and books. Though they do not intend to be offensive, TS patients may make obscene gestures like "giving the finger," or they may imitate any movements or gestures made by others.
- Simple vocal tics. These include clearing the throat, coughing, snorting, barking, grunting, yelping, and clicking the tongue. Patients may screech or make whistling, hissing, or sucking sounds. They may repeat sounds such as "uh, uh," or "eee."

• Complex vocal tics and patterns. Older children with TS may repeat a phrase such as "Oh boy," "All right," or "What's that?" Or they may repeat everything they, or others, say a certain number of times. Some patients speak very rapidly or loudly, or in a strange tone or accent. Coprolalia (saying "dirty words" or suggestive or hostile phrases) is probably the best known feature of TS, but fewer than one-third of all patients display this symptom.

Behavioral abnormalities that may be associated with TS include attention deficit hyperactivity disorder (ADHD) and disruptive behaviors, including conduct disorder and oppositional defiant disorder, with aggressive, destructive, antisocial, or negativistic behavior. Academic disorders, learning disorders, and sleep abnormalities (such as sleepwalking and nightmares) are also seen in TS patients.

Diagnosis

There are no specific tests for TS. TS is diagnosed by observing the symptoms and asking whether relatives have had a similar condition. To qualify as TS, both motor and vocal tics should be present for at least a year and should begin before age 18 (or, some believe, age 21). Often, the diagnosis is delayed because the patient is misunderstood not only at home and at school, but in the doctor's office as well. It may take some time for the patient to trust the doctor enough not to suppress the strangest or most alarming tics. Blood tests may be done in some cases to rule out other movement disorders. A test of the brain's electrical activity (electroencephalograph or EEG) is often abnormal in TS, but not specific. A thorough medication history is very important in making the diagnosis as well, because stimulant drugs may provoke tics or aggravate the symptoms of TS.

Various Therapies

Although there is no cure for TS, many alternative treatments may lessen the severity and frequency of the tics. These include:

- Acupuncture. In one study, acupuncture treatment of 156 children with TS had a 92.3% effective rate.
- Behavioral treatments. Some of these can help TS patients control tics. A large variety of these methods exist, some with proven success.
- Cognitive behavioral therapy. This form of therapy helps the patient to change his or her ingrained response to a particular stimulus. It is somewhat effective in treating the obsessive-compulsive behaviors associated with TS.
- Neurofeedback (electroencephalographic biofeedback). In neurofeedback, the patient learns to control brain wave patterns; it may be effective in reducing the symptoms of TS. There are, however, no data on this modality as a treatment for TS.
- Psychotherapy. This form of treatment can help the TS patient, and his or her family, cope with depression, poor relationships, and other issues commonly associated with TS.
- Relaxation techniques. Yoga and progressive muscular relaxation are believed to help TS, especially when used in combination with other treatments, because they lower the patient's stress level. One small study found that relaxation therapy (awareness training, deep breathing, behavioral relaxation training, applied relaxation techniques, and biofeedback) reduced the severity of tics, although the difference between the treatment group and control group was not statistically significant.
- Stress reduction training. This training may help relieve the symptoms of TS because stress worsens the tics.

• Other alternative therapies. Homeopathy, hypnosis, guided imagery, and eliminating allergy-provoking foods from the diet have all been reported as helping some TS patients.

Drugs and Other Treatments

Most TS patients do not need to take drugs, as their tics do not seriously interfere with their lives. Drugs that are used to reduce the symptoms of TS include haloperidol (Haldol), pimozide (Orap), clonidine (Catapres), guanfacine (Tenex), and risperidone (Risperdal). One interesting recent finding is that the transdermal nicotine patch, developed to help people quit smoking, improves the control of TS symptoms in children who take haloperidol. Use of the patch allows the haloperidol dosage to be cut in half without loss of effectiveness in symptom control.

Stereotactic treatment, which is high-frequency stimulation of specific regions of the brain, was reported to be successful in significantly reducing tics in a TS patient who had failed to respond to other treatments.

Although there is no cure for TS, many patients improve as they grow older, often to the point where they can manage their lives without drugs. A few patients recover completely after their teenage years. Others learn to live with their condition. There is always a risk, however, that a patient who continues having severe tics will become more antisocial or depressed, or develop severe mood swings and panic attacks.

The only way to prevent TS is for a couple not to have children when one of them has the condition. Any child of a TS parent has a 50% chance of inheriting the syndrome.

Tics and Tourette Syndrome Are Common Childhood Conditions

Leslie E. Packer

Leslie E. Packer is a New York psychologist and consultant who treats individuals with Tourette syndrome (TS), obsessive-compulsive disorder, and related conditions. She is also a coauthor *of Challenging Kids, Challenged Teachers*, a book about teaching children with multiple neurological disorders, and author of *Find a Way or Make a Way,* a book containing hundreds of accommodation tips and strategies, sorted by the type of challenges the students face. In this selection Packer maintains that nearly 20 percent of all children experience tics—involuntary movements or sounds—at some point in their development. Tics are not always indicative of TS; some children have "transient" tic conditions that do not require treatment, and there are other non-TS conditions that produce tics. A person might be diagnosed with TS if he or she has multiple motor tics and at least one vocal tic that occur in waxing and waning cycles for more than a year, Packer explains. However, numerous cases of TS go undiagnosed.

Many people with TS are able to suppress their tics to a certain degree—especially if they are engaged in an engrossing activity—but at some point tics need to be released. Youths who put effort

SOURCE: Leslie E. Packer, "Tics and Tourette Syndrome: Overview," SchoolBehavior.com, 2011. All rights reserved. Reproduced by permission.

into suppressing their tics all day at school often have an explosion of tics upon returning home. Tics can negatively affect academic performance and social relationships, but they have their greatest impact on a student's self-esteem. Packer often encourages schools to place TS students in enrichment or gifted programs that encourage concentration and focus.

A tic is a brief, repetitive, purposeless, nonrhythmic, involuntary movement or sound. Tics that produce movement are called "motor tics," while tics that produce sound are called "vocal tics" or "phonic tics." Motor tics seems to be more common than vocal tics.

Tics are often characterized by whether they are "simple" or "complex." A simple tic involves one muscle group or one simple sound. Many simple motor tics are associated with the face/head/neck region, such as eye blinking, head jerking, shoulder shrugging, mouth grimacing, etc. Simple vocal tics include throat-clearing sounds, grunting, sniffing, and coughing. Simple motor tics of the face and head/neck region are the most common first tics in children.

A complex tic involves a coordinated movement produced by a number of muscle groups (complex motor tic) or a linguistically meaningful utterance or phrase (complex vocal tic). As examples, complex motor tics can involve touching objects or other people, jumping up and down, spinning around, or even more complex motor sequences such as imitating someone else's actions (echopraxia) or exhibiting inappropriate or taboo gestures or behaviors (copropraxia). Complex vocal tics may involve having to repeat one phrase over and over, whether it is something one heard (echolalia) or one's own last words (palilalia).

Many Children Experience Tics

A significant percentage of all children will experience one, or even a few, tics at some point in their development. For most children, a tic will emerge without any warning or explanation, remain a few weeks, and then disappear slowly. Over 18% of all children have one or more tics at some point in their development.

If tic(s) are present for less than a year and do not recur, we say that the child has a "transient" tic condition. The transient tic condition observed in children is generally benign and usually does not require treatment.

If there is a history of a number of tics that have been present—even if not continuously—for more than a year, we say that there is a "chronic" tic condition. A chronic motor tic condition is one in which the individual has one or several motor tics (but no vocal tics) on and off for more than a year, while a chronic vocal tic condition is one in which there has been one or more vocal tics (but no motor tics) on and off for more than a year.

If the individual has a history of a number of motor tics and at least one vocal tic, and tics have been present on and off for more than a year and there has been a pattern where the tics emerge, get worse over weeks, then ease up, then the individual may have Tourette's Syndrome (TS). The word "may" is important, because there are other conditions that could produce multiple tics without the individual having Tourette's Syndrome. There are no brain or blood tests that can definitely prove a child or teen has TS: the diagnosis is a clinical one, based on history, observation, and reports.

Identifying Tourette's Syndrome

Approximately 3% of children in regular education classrooms may have Tourette's Syndrome; more than 7% of children in special education have Tourette's Syndrome. The majority of these children have never been diagnosed.

In the majority of cases, the first tics of Tourette's Syndrome are usually simple motor tics of the head, face, neck, and shoulder region or simple phonic tics. Eye blinking is the most common "first tic," but it is important to

Tic Classification

Simple Tics	Motor Tics	Eye blinking, grimacing, head twisting, tongue clicking
	Phonic Tics	Repetitve throat clearing, sniffing, snorting, grunting
Complex Tics	Motor Tics	Hopping, jumping, grimacing while twisting head, touching objects
	Phonic Tics	Strings of words, phrases, coprolalia, echolalia

Taken from: "Tourette's Syndrome." *DBS: Deep Brain Stimulation*, 2008. biomed.brown.edu.

remember that having this tic does not necessarily indicate that the child will develop Tourette's, as approximately 1 in every 5 children will have a tic at some point in their development.

The first tics of TS are often erroneously thought to be "nervous habits," allergies, or unexplained colds. For example, a child who suddenly starts sniffing may be thought to have a cold or allergies, but the pediatrician may find no evidence of a cold and no clear allergy symptoms such as rhinitis. Similarly, a child who suddenly starts blinking their eyes a lot may be thought to have some vision problem or allergies, but on examination, there will be no evidence to support the notion that the blinking is allergy-related.

In most cases, after a tic first appears, it will increase in frequency and severity for a few weeks to a month or so, and then start to subside. Eventually, it usually disappears completely. Unless the parents or teachers are already aware of a history of tic disorders in the family or are familiar with tics or Tourette's Syndrome from other sources, the first tics are not likely to be recognized as tics.

Following the disappearance of the first tic (or tics), a few months may go by and then the tic may re-emerge or a new tic may appear. The tic (or tics) will increase in frequency and severity over weeks and then subside and disappear.

While the average age of onset of TS is 6–7 years old, there are many cases where parents later realized that their child's tics had actually started much younger. In almost all cases, TS emerges before age 18, but there are exceptions. In some children, TS may emerge more forcefully or explosively. A child with no recognized history of tics may suddenly erupt in a number of tics within a very short period, or the child may present with complex tics instead of simple tics. Another situation in which severe tics or symptoms may emerge is those cases that appear to be related to infections

Can Tics Be Supressed?

Even though tics are considered to be "involuntary" or "unvoluntary," many individuals report a sensory basis for their tics—they feel the need to tic building up as a kind of tension in a particular anatomical location, and they feel that they consciously choose to release it. The sensations and internal events leading up to the expression of the tic are often referred to in the literature as "premonitory sensory phenomena." Young children are often unaware of their tics and generally do not report such premonitory urges. The awareness of the premonitory phenomenon seems to take a developmental leap around age 14.

Tics can sometimes be suppressed, but most people's experience is that the tics will eventually be released. Thus, if we were to ask someone who felt that the tics were consciously released to not tic, we might observe that they could suppress a tic for a while, but eventually, they would release it. As one child put it, "I can stop ticcing when you can stop breathing." Developmentally, the child's ability to suppress tics seems to increase around age 10, although any one child may not have much ability to suppress any tic for any length of time.

What happens if the individual tries to suppress the tics? Some individuals have no control at all over their tics, while others have varying degrees of control. Most adults report that their ability to modify or suppress their tics improved as they matured.

With young children, it is important to remember that the child may not be aware of their tics, and even if they are aware, they may have no ability to suppress them. Asking a child who has tics to suppress them is generally not a good idea because:

- the effort involved in suppressing the tics will distract the child from whatever else is going on that they should be paying attention to, and
- the effort spent in suppressing tics is stressful and can produce fatigue and/or irritability, and when the tics are eventually released, they may be more explosive.

It is a common phenomenon that children or adolescents who try to suppress their tics in school all day (with varying degrees of success) will come home from school, walk in the door, and explode in tics—often accompanied by a lot of emotional behaviors.

Cycles of Tics

As noted earlier, tics tend to come in bursts or "bouts." The child or adolescent may have a bout of ticcing, followed by a period of calm, and then another bout of ticcing. Dr. James Leckman talks about this pattern as being one of "bouts within bouts within bouts," whereby bursts of ties may be experienced throughout the day, over days, over weeks and months.

When the number of bouts within the day is increasing, we say that the child is in a "waxing" cycle. As the number of bouts within the day or over days decreases, we say that they are in a "waning" cycle. These waxing and waning cycles are a hallmark of TS.

How does a particular bout end, however? For many individuals with Tourette's, there is a sense that the tic needs to be performed or released until they achieve a "just so" kind of sensation or experience. An analogy might be to think of the last time that you had a mosquito bite. You became aware of the itch and need to scratch. You may have been able to delay scratching or to try to substitute scratching near the bite instead of directly on it, but you continued doing something until the itch was relieved or you got some "just right" sensation—either a feeling in the skin or the sight of blood let you know that you could stop. The sensory phenomena and the "just so" or "just right" kind of tic experience seem to be more common in patients who have Tourette's or Tourette's plus Obsessive-Compulsive Disorder than in patients who have just Obsessive-Compulsive Disorder.

Based on research and clinical experience, however, it is important to note that although about 10% of all

Approximately 3 percent of children in regular education classes may have Tourette syndrome, and more than 7 percent of children in special education have the disorder. (© **Enigma/Alamy**)

children with TS will have "just TS," the vast majority will have one or more other conditions as well. . . .

Long-Term Prognosis

Most cases of TS are thought to be "mild," meaning that the individual does not seek treatment and/or does not experience significant interference in their life from their tics. If tics become problematic, there are a variety of medications that may provide some relief from the tics and at least one empirically validated non-medication treatment for tics.

In the first years after onset, many people report that the waxing periods tend to worsen from one waxing cycle to the next. The child may experience more tics and/or more severe tics over time, and there seems to be a tendency for things to get worse before they get better. The good news is that for many (but not all) individuals, the tics will ease up significantly or go into remission in the teen years. A report by [James] Leckman et al. suggests that tics seem to reach their peak severity between the ages of 10–12 in the majority of cases, and that by age 18, half of the children may be virtually tic-free, with other children showing significant improvement.

Impact of Tics on School Functioning

Based mainly on parental surveys, anecdotal reports, and my own experiences as a psychologist and parent, it appears that tics may directly impact academic functioning in the following ways:

- Simple motor tics of the eyes, head, and neck region may interfere with reading activities.
- Simple motor tics may also interfere with handwriting activities.
- Children with vocal tics may be reluctant to read aloud in front of their peers or may hesitate to ask questions in class.

The above are just some examples that have been noted by parents and individuals with TS, and are not intended as an exhaustive list of possible types of interference. While we should never assume that a child's tics are creating interference for him or her, an informed teacher can be alert to possible interference or distress and the need for some accommodations.

Do children with TS have a greater risk of learning disabilities? Because some studies have not isolated children with TS-only from those with TS-ADHD [Tourette syndrome–attention-deficit/hyperactivity disorder], it's not yet clear whether TS by itself actually increases the risk for a learning disability [LD], although some sources would indicate that students with TS are more likely to have math and written expressive LDs than their non-TS peers. If the child with TS does have ADHD as well, there is an increased risk of learning disabilities and a significantly increased risk of referral for special education.

In general, children with uncomplicated TS (TS-only) are more likely than their non-TS peers to have problems with visual-motor integration, which may impact handwriting and copying from the blackboard. They may also need more time and/or testing accommodations due to interference from tics. Given a supportive environment that makes reasonable accommodations and that provides support for peer issues, children with uncomplicated TS should be able to learn and perform commensurate with their non-TS peers. When the child with TS also has ADHD, however, the ADHD is a significant predictor of school-related problems.

In an Internet survey, Packer asked parents or guardians of children and adolescents with Tourette's to assess the impact of tics on academic functioning, peer relationships, and other activities. While the majority reported at least some impact on academic functioning and peer

FAST FACT

Baseball player and TS patient Jim Eisenreich, former hitter and outfielder for the Philadelphia Phillies, experienced tics in front of thousands of fans.

interactions, the greatest impact of tics appeared to be on the child's self-esteem about school and on family functioning.

The notion that tics could lead to impaired peer relationships has some support in a number of published studies that indicate that children and teens with Tourette's are more likely to experience peer rejection due to their tics. Even those students who "only" have tics may need your support to develop normal peer relationships.

Other factors can also influence the frequency or severity of tics:

Factors That Increase Tics:	Factors That Decrease Tics:
• Time pressure	• Distracted
• Stress	• Non-anxiously engrossed
• Arousal	• During skilled tasks
• Before and after performing skilled tasks	• During sleep
• Starting to relax	• Summer vacation
• Fatigued	• Waning cycle
• Waxing cycle	• Nicotine
• Illness (infections)	• Asked to suppress tics (initial response)
• Allergies	• Novel situation
• Caffeine	• Doctor's examining room
• Environmental heat	
• Premenstrual period	
• Asked to suppress tics (delayed reaction)	
• Talking to the student about their tics	

Variability in Tics and Symptom Severity

One phenomenon that has often been reported is that under some conditions, children may not tic at all. As just one example, children who might be ticcing quite a bit may not tic at all in the doctor's office. Similarly, they may exhibit very few tics in school, due to either involuntary suppression or voluntary attempts to suppress their tics. Those who are not knowledgeable about tics or Tourette's generally misinterpret this phenomenon to mean that tics are more controllable than they actually are.

When someone who has Tourette's is totally and constructively engrossed in something, the tics may stop altogether. This is not generally experienced as a stressful form of suppression, and suggests an important strategy for working with students in the classroom:

If they are ticcing a lot, and you present something that is novel and fascinating to them, their tics will probably just stop as their neurochemistry shifts in response to the novel situation or activity. If they are having a really rough time from tics, consider giving them an opportunity to engage in an activity that will be engrossing for them.

Because children who tic actually tend to tic less when they are fascinated with classroom tasks or activities, the author has often encouraged schools to put the student in enrichment or gifted programs that are more likely to enable them to focus constructively.

Coprolalia: The Cursing Tic

Lawrence Scahill

In the following selection Lawrence Scahill examines coprolalia, a complex vocal tic in which one unintentionally repeats socially unacceptable words. Coprolalia was once thought to be the primary symptom of Tourette syndrome (TS), but today's experts maintain that this tic affects a minority of TS patients. Coprolalia is probably caused by the body's failure to inhibit signals in multiple pathways in the brain, Scahill points out. Tic-suppressing medications have produced mixed results in reducing coprolalia.

Since coprolalia is often preceded by a feeling or warning prior to its verbal expression, some people who have this tic can learn to replace swear words with less-offensive terms, the author maintains. TS patients can also reduce the social impact of coprolalia by identifying the situations in which the tic is more likely to occur and developing strategies specific to those situations. Scahill is a professor of nursing and child psychiatry at Yale University in New Haven, Connecticut.

SOURCE: Lawrence Scahill, "Ask the Expert," *Inside TSA*, Tourette Syndrome Association, Spring 2008, p. 5.

W *hat is coprolalia and what is the cause?* Coprolalia is a complex vocal tic that occurs when a person involuntarily repeats curse words, makes reference to male or female body parts, utters racial epithets or other socially inappropriate vocalizations.

These unfortunate outbursts are by no means an indication of a person's personal beliefs. In the past, coprolalia was considered to be the defining feature of TS [Tourette syndrome]. Today, we no longer believe that having this symptom is necessary in order to confirm a TS diagnosis. Indeed, experienced clinicians agree that coprolalia is relatively uncommon among people with TS. This change in viewpoint is a reflection of the gradual broadening of the very definition of TS. Although it is not uniformly the case, coprolalia does tend to occur in those with the more severe forms of TS symptoms.

The cause of coprolalia is not known. However, the tics of TS—even simple tics—may challenge the boundary between what is voluntary and what is involuntary. This challenge is even greater when we try to understand more complex tics such as coprolalia.

The Need to Tic

Many, in fact most individuals with TS describe a feeling or an urge prior to performing some or all of their tics. Some will go even further and report that the feeling or urge actually drives the need to tic. They tell us that "If I didn't have the urge, I wouldn't have the tics." Generally, tics appear to be caused by a failure to inhibit signals in motor pathways in the brain. These pathways can be thought of as circuits or loops involving both sensory inputs (perhaps the source of premonitory urges) and motor outputs (movements). The actual physical location of the tic (e.g., facial movement, head jerk, shoulder shrug, throat clearing) may reflect the specific brain circuit where this failure of inhibition occurs. In other words, the reason why some people have facial tics and others have head jerks or throat clearing may have to do with the specific brain circuit that is not properly regulated. Putting this all together, we can imagine a person with TS feeling tension in the neck, followed very soon thereafter with a head jerking tic. There may be momentary relief from the tension—only to have it return again, and then the cycle repeats. Despite the very brief warning or feeling prior to the tic, we regard the movement as being involuntary because the person cannot stop the tic from occurring. In other words, an awareness that the tic is about to be expressed does not mean that the person can stop it from happening.

This model works pretty well for understanding simple motor and vocal tics. When it comes to complicated ones such as combination tics (e.g., a head jerk followed by an arm jerk and a grunting sound) or coprolalia, it gets—well—complicated. Once again, often people report a feeling or warning prior to executing a verbal outburst. Given that coprolalia involves motor output (muscles used in speech) and the production of a word that has meaning and that is socially inappropriate—it seems likely that more than one brain pathway or circuit is involved.

Tic-Suppressing Tactics

Is there a medication strategy that is effective for reducing coprolalia? Unfortunately, it is unlikely that a medication—even one that has proved effective in reducing tics—will have specific benefits to reduce the symptoms of coprolalia. Indeed, the use of tic suppressing medications to treat any single tic is often unsatisfactory. This is because the currently available effective medications rarely take away all tics. Rather, effective medications tend to turn down the overall severity of tics but may not result in the elimination of specific tics. If the medication does succeed in doing away with a specific tic, still there is no way of knowing at the start of treatment which one will be reduced or eliminated. That said, this does not mean that medication should not be tried in patients with coprolalia. It just

"He has a variant of Tourette's Syndrome that's been around since the Middle Ages."

"He has a variant of Tourette's Syndrome that's been around since the Middle Ages," cartoon by RGJ—Richard Jolley. Www.CartoonStock.com.

means that expectations should not be unduly optimistic about the impact of medication on any single tic—including coprolalia.

Can a person substitute something that is more acceptable in place of the curse word or inappropriate expression? Some individuals discover on their own that they can alter a specific tic in a way that decreases the socially inappropriate quality of coprolalia. For example, a patient may substitute "Ford Focus" for the "F word" or "biscuit" for the "B word."

To help patients with this strategy, often it is useful to look closely at the specific situations when coprolalia occurs. In some cases, for example, this assessment will show that a person engages in this behavior when angry, or when under some pressure or when excited. When considering any of these patterns, we might ask whether the behavior is a tic or a problem of impulse control during periods of frustration or excitement. For example, I received an urgent call from a school principal about an 11-year-old boy who was running through the playground during recess blurting out curse words. The profanity was directed to several fifth grade girls. After discussions with the family, the child and school personnel, it became clear that indeed this boy had motor and vocal tics and was properly diagnosed with TS. However, among his TS symptoms there had been no other hint of his having coprolalia. Based on the assumption that this behavior was not a TS tic, we developed a plan to deal with this unacceptable behavior and it stopped within days.

> **FAST FACT**
>
> Coprolalia affects about one out of every ten people with TS.

Preventative Strategies

Even when careful assessment results in the conclusion that the cursing is a TS tic, it is still likely that the inappropriate vocalizations will occur in some situations more often than others. Pinpointing the situations when the behavior is most likely to occur can be used to develop more specific strategies than simply saying: "try not to do it" or "whenever you get the urge, go to the Time Out room." For example, if the behavior occurs primarily at school, school personnel and classmates can be educated to tolerate the behavior—at least within certain limits. If the behavior goes beyond the agreed upon limits, the child can be excused from the classroom to minimize disruption. It may also be possible to develop preventive strategies together with the child. These strategies are based on the explicit understanding that the cursing is a tic and that the child is not to be blamed for the behavior. Nonetheless, clinicians, parents and the child can agree that a plan is needed to reduce the potential negative social impact of the behavior. In some cases, solutions might be relatively obvious. For example, I recall a case of a teenage boy who shouted out racial epithets at his high school basketball games. In the

Some people with Tourette syndrome experience coprolalia when angry, under presure, or excited. (© Oscar Burriel/Photo Researchers, Inc.)

short run, it made sense to stop going to the games. This interim solution did not emerge until it became clear that this was indeed a "high risk" situation. His coprolalia did occur in other low impact settings, but no specific interventions were required for these situations. As with many tics, his coprolalia subsided over time and eventually the boy was able to return to athletic events without incidents. In another case, knowledge of the situation when the unwanted tic is most likely to occur may lead to the strategy of substituting the curse word with a similar sounding— but more socially appropriate word.

Tourette Syndrome May Occur with Related Conditions

Centers for Disease Control and Prevention

A branch of the US Department of Health and Human Services, the Centers for Disease Control and Prevention (CDC) develops strategies to fight disease and designs educational activities to help improve the health of the US population. In the following selection the CDC provides an overview of other behavioral and mental health conditions that are frequently seen in people with Tourette syndrome (TS). For example, attention-deficit/hyperactivity disorder (ADHD), a condition that leads to poor impulse control and difficulty with concentration, occurs in a majority of children with TS. Other conditions sometimes seen with TS include obsessive-compulsive disorder, oppositional defiant disorder, anxiety, and depression. While people with TS and related disorders have normal levels of intelligence, they may be challenged in school environments if they have problems with organization or paying attention. The CDC suggests that schools provide additional accommodations and behavioral interventions for students with TS.

Tourette Syndrome (TS) often occurs with other related conditions (also called co-occurring conditions). These conditions can include attention-deficit/hyperactivity disorder (ADHD), obsessive-compulsive disorder (OCD), and other behavioral or conduct problems. People with TS and related conditions can be at higher risk for learning, behavioral, and social problems.

The symptoms of other disorders can complicate the diagnosis and treatment of TS and create extra challenges for people with TS and their families, educators, and health professionals.

Findings from a national Centers for Disease Control and Prevention (CDC) study indicated that 79% of children who had been diagnosed with TS also had been diagnosed with at least one additional mental health, behavioral, or developmental condition.

Among children with TS:

- 64% had ADHD.
- 43% had behavioral problems, such as oppositional defiant disorder (ODD) or conduct disorder (CD).
- 40% had anxiety problems.
- 36% had depression.
- 28% had a developmental delay.

Because co-occurring conditions are so common among people with TS, it is important for doctors to assess every child with TS for other conditions and problems.

Attention-Deficit/Hyperactivity Disorder (ADHD)

In a national CDC study, ADHD was the most common co-occurring condition among children with TS. Of children who had been diagnosed with TS, 64% also had been diagnosed with ADHD.

Children with ADHD have trouble paying attention and controlling impulsive behaviors. They might act

Tourette Syndrome and Co-Occurring Conditions

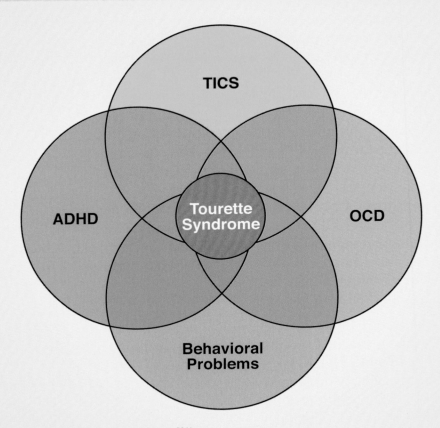

Taken from: www.health-reply.com, January 2011.

without thinking about what the result will be and, in some cases, they are also overly active. It is normal for children to have trouble focusing and behaving at one time or another. However, these behaviors continue beyond early childhood (0–5 years of age) among children with ADHD. Symptoms of ADHD can continue and can cause difficulty at school, at home, or with friends.

Obsessive-Compulsive Behaviors

People with obsessive-compulsive behaviors have unwanted thoughts (obsessions) that they feel a need to respond to (compulsions). Obsessive-compulsive behaviors and obsessive-compulsive disorder (OCD) have been shown to occur among more than one-third of people with TS. Sometimes it is difficult to tell the difference between complex tics that a child with TS may have and obsessive-compulsive behaviors.

Behavior or Conduct Problems

Findings from the CDC study indicated that behavior or conduct problems, such as oppositional defiant disorder (ODD) or conduct disorder (CD), had been diagnosed among 43% of children with TS.

Oppositional Defiant Disorder (ODD). People with ODD show negative, defiant and hostile behaviors toward adults or authority figures. ODD usually starts before a child is 8 years of age, but no later than early adolescence. Symptoms might occur most often with people the individual knows well, such as family members or a regular care provider. The behaviors associated with ODD are present beyond what might be expected for the person's age, and result in major problems in school, at home, or with peers.

Examples of ODD behaviors include:

- Losing one's temper a lot.
- Arguing with adults or refusing to comply with adults' rules or requests.
- Getting angry or being resentful or vindictive often.
- Annoying others on purpose or easily becoming annoyed with others.
- Blaming other people often for one's own mistakes or misbehavior.

Conduct Disorder (CD). People with CD have aggression toward others and break rules, laws, and social norms. Increased injuries and difficulty with friends also are common among people with CD. In addition, the symptoms of CD happen in more than one area in the person's life (for example, at home, in the community, and at school).

CD is severe and highly disruptive to a person's life and to others in his or her life. It also is very challenging to treat. If a person has CD it is important to get a diagnosis and treatment plan from a mental health professional as soon as possible.

Rage. Some people with TS have anger that is out of control, or episodes of "rage." Rage is not a disorder that can be diagnosed. Symptoms of rage might include extreme verbal or physical aggression. Examples of verbal aggression include extreme yelling, screaming, and cursing. Examples of physical aggression include extreme shoving, kicking, hitting, biting, and throwing objects. Rage symptoms are more likely to occur among those with other behavioral disorders such as ADHD, ODD, or CD.

Among people with TS, symptoms of rage are more likely to occur at home than outside the home. Treatment of rage can include learning how to relax, social skills training, and therapy. Some of these methods will help individuals and families better understand what can cause the rage, how to avoid encouraging these behaviors, and how to use appropriate discipline for these behaviors. In addition, treating other behavioral disorders that the person might have, such as ADHD, ODD, or CD can help to reduce symptoms of rage.

FAST FACT

The National Institute of Mental Health states that children with TS may develop different patterns of brain activity in order to function at the same level as children without TS.

Anxiety

There are many different types of anxiety disorders with many different causes and symptoms. These include generalized anxiety disorder, OCD, panic disorder, posttraumatic stress disorder, separation anxiety, and different types of phobias. Separation anxiety is most common among young children. These children feel very worried when they are apart from their parents.

Depression

Everyone feels worried, anxious, sad, or stressed from time to time. However, if these feelings do not go away and they interfere with daily life (for example, keeping a child home from school or other activities, or keeping an adult from working or attending social activities), a person might have depression. Having either a depressed mood or a loss of interest or pleasure for at least two weeks might mean that someone has depression. Children and teens with depression might be irritable instead of sad.

To be diagnosed with depression, other symptoms also must be present, such as:

- Changes in eating habits or weight gain or loss.
- Changes in sleep habits.
- Changes in activity level (others notice increased activity or that the person has slowed down).
- Less energy.

Sixty-four percent of children with Tourette syndrome also have attention-deficit/hyperactivity disorder (ADHD). (© Leila Cutler/Alamy)

- Feelings of worthlessness or guilt.
- Difficulty thinking, concentrating, or making decisions.
- Repeated thoughts of death.
- Thoughts or plans about suicide, or a suicide attempt.
- Depression can be treated with counseling and medication.

Educational Concerns

As a group, people with TS have levels of intelligence similar to those of people without TS. However, people with TS might be more likely to have learning differences, a learning disability, or a developmental delay that affects their ability to learn.

Many people with TS have problems with writing, organizing, and paying attention. People with TS might have problems processing what they hear or see. This can affect the person's ability to learn by listening to or watching a teacher. Or, the person might have problems with their other senses (such as how things feel, smell, taste, and movement) that affects learning and behavior. Children with TS might have trouble with social skills that affect their ability to interact with others.

As a result of these challenges, children with TS might need extra help in school. Many times, these concerns can be addressed with accommodations and behavioral interventions (for example, help with social skills).

Accommodations can include things such as providing a different testing location or extra testing time, providing tips on how to be more organized, giving the child less homework, or letting the child use a computer to take notes in class. Children also might need behavioral interventions, therapy, or they may need to learn strategies to help with stress, paying attention, or other symptoms.

CHAPTER 2

Controversies Surrounding Tourette Syndrome

Various Drugs Can Help Control Tourette Syndrome

David Shprecher and Roger Kurlan

In the following selection David Shprecher and Roger Kurlan discuss some pharmaceutical approaches to treating Tourette syndrome. Initially, symptoms must be evaluated by examining a medical history and defining any potential contributors to the problem, such as co-occurring disorders. By doing so, a physician can more accurately target the most troubling symptoms for therapy. Educating the parents, teachers, and peers of the patient is also an important early step, as a supportive environment leads to improved outcomes. Drugs frequently used to suppress tics include alpha-agonists, dopamine-blocking agents, and antipsychotics. In some cases injections of botulinum toxin can reduce the urge to tic. Potential alternative medicines for tics include cannabis and androgen blockers. Shprecher is an assistant professor of neurology at the University of Utah School of Medicine in Salt Lake City. Kurlan is a professor of neurology at the University of Rochester School of Medicine and Dentistry in New York.

Photo on previous page. A boy with Tourette syndrome participates in dolphin therapy. (© John Chapple/Getty Images)

SOURCE: David Shprecher and Roger Kurlan, "The Management of Tics," *Movement Disorders,* v. 24, no. 1, January 15, 2009, pp. 15–24. All rights reserved. Reproduced by permission.

Chronic tics are the characteristic feature of Tourette's syndrome (TS). Diagnostic criteria include presence of both motor and vocal tics, onset in childhood, fluctuations in tic types and severity, and duration of at least one year. When chronic tics of both types cannot be identified, the terms chronic motor tic disorder and chronic vocal tic disorder are used. Tics lasting less than 1 year are termed transient tic disorder. With very high comorbidity rates of both attention deficit hyperactivity disorder (ADHD) and obsessive-compulsive disorder (OCD), TS may represent a multifaceted developmental neuropsychiatric brain disorder.

TS is thought to result from a developmental failure of inhibitory function within the frontal-subcortical circuits governing voluntary movements, possibly leading to impaired surround-off inhibition (the ability to suppress unwanted movements). Dysfunction of dopamine neurotransmission is strongly implicated in this process, with current evidence pointing to low tonic synaptic dopamine levels and excessive phasic release of dopamine in the basal ganglia. Some neuroimaging evidence suggests an increase in presynaptic dopamine transporters or excessive dopaminergic innervation. . . .

Initial Evaluation

The management of tics is made challenging by a general lack of definitive evidence to support or refute commonly used treatments. This review is drawn from a synthesis of existing research data and the authors' personal experience in this area. A thorough clinical history and neurologic examination are generally sufficient to screen for evidence of a secondary tic disorder, and neuroimaging or electroencephalography are usually not needed unless there are unexpected findings. A more global developmental process may be suggested by history of early neurologic insults, a delay in developmental milestones, or the occurrence of seizures. A critical aspect of the initial evaluation is to check for the presence and severity of commonly associated neuropsychiatric disorders, ADHD, and OCD. We also ask about a family history of tics, ADHD, and OCD. Mood disorders, other anxiety disorders, impulse control problems, and rage attacks should also be assessed. It is also important to know about psychosocial stressors. The important goal is to accurately define the contributors to existing problems. For example, problems with attention in school could be related to ADHD, medication side effects, mental fatigue caused by efforts to suppress tics, obsessive thinking, anxiety, depression, or a learning disability. An important component of the history is to determine which symptoms are disabling (ie, causing problems in daily functioning) in order to select those target symptoms appropriate for therapy.

Educating the Patient, Family, and School

Education of parents, teachers, and peers is a critical initial intervention. We inform patients and their parents that it is appropriate to tell others that they have tics, meaning that they cannot help making certain movements or sounds. We provide patients and parents with current information about the causes of tics (genetic factors, brain neurochemical imbalances) and emphasize that they are not signs of psychological or emotional illness, a common misperception. Learning about the importance of genetic factors often relieves a sense of guilt in the patient and parent. Although serious psychosocial factors can exacerbate tics, we explain how tics change in type over time and that they naturally fluctuate in severity, so it is not necessary to search for psychological problems every time their child experiences more tics. We explain the process of voluntary suppression and emphasize there is no value for anyone to point out tics to the child or tell them to stop their tics. What is needed is

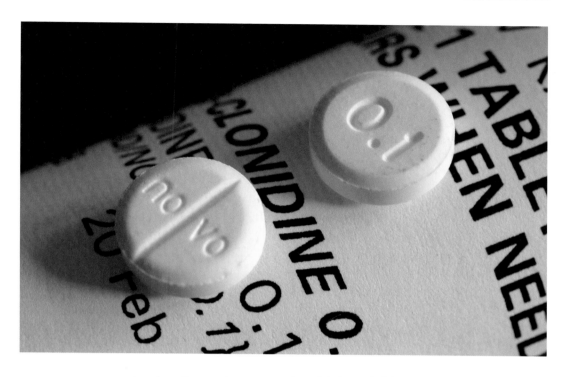

Clonidine is used for a variety of maladies, including Tourette syndrome. (© Scimat/ Photo Researchers, Inc.)

an open, supportive family environment in which a child can comfortably approach their parents to let them know about problematic tics or other symptoms.

A majority of TS patients experience improvement of tics in late adolescence or early adulthood. This is an important piece of information that patients and families should receive so they understand that the prognosis of TS can be quite good. We generally educate the family about the "clinical triad" (tics, ADHD, and OCD) of TS and discuss how these features relate to the patient and are often seen in relatives. We explain that the presence of tics or related symptoms per se is not a reason to initiate medication therapy or another therapeutic intervention. The key decision-making element is whether a symptom is causing significant problems in daily functioning.

Education is often needed for school personnel because there are many misperceptions of tics as being voluntary, attention-seeking, or purposely disruptive behaviors. Educating classmates may be needed and trained professionals are available in many areas to assist with this. Useful educational videos and other materials are available from the Tourette Syndrome Association (www.tsa-usa.org). Because tics can occasionally be disruptive or distract other children, we recommend that special accommodations be considered in the school setting. These might include excusing the child, at his or her request, to the nurse's office to release tics or providing additional time in a separate room when taking school tests. Such provisions are mandated in [the] United States under laws protecting individuals with disabilities.

Initial Treatment Considerations

The critical first step in making treatment decisions in patients with TS is to select the most appropriate target symptoms, the ones causing the most problems in a patient's daily functioning. In one patient it may be the tics themselves, in another it may be comorbid ADHD or OCD and in another it may be a combination of targets. Because psychosocial stresses can worsen symptoms, it is important to probe for these and consider interventions such as individual or family counseling. For patients with mild symptoms, educational and psychological interventions may be sufficient to bring symptoms to a tolerable level of severity. Symptoms that continue to cause disability are then appropriate for medication therapy. It is important to focus on the patient's disability and not to treat just because parents find their child's tics or other symptoms to be annoying or embarrassing. Clinicians should remember that tics characteristically wax and wane in severity, so sometimes just waiting for some period of time can result in a lessening of tics and avoid medication use or increases.

FAST FACT

Alpha-agonist drugs such as clonidine are commonly used to treat high blood pressure but can also help reduce tics associated with Tourette syndrome.

We generally treat tics that interfere with school or other daily activities, or are disabling because of social embarrassment, physical discomfort, or self-injury. In prescribing tic-suppressing medications, we usually titrate dosage to identify the lowest one that will result in resolution of disability. In considering the evidence supporting the efficacy of tic-suppressing drugs it is important to recognize that a substantial placebo response has been documented.

Alpha-2-Agonists

Alpha-2-agonists have moderate efficacy for tics. Although clonidine was the alpha agonist most commonly used in the past, guanfacine is now preferred because it tends to cause less sedation and can usually be dosed once (bedtime) or twice (morning, bedtime) compared with the three to four daily doses needed for clonidine. Guanfacine also tends to produce less sedation. The clonidine transdermal patch may be useful for young children who cannot swallow pills. The most common potential side effects of guanfacine include sedation, headache, dizziness, irritability, and dry mouth. We have seen a few patients who experienced syncope [loss of consciousness] while treated with guanfacine. Alpha agonists are a particularly good choice for patients with tics and ADHD (see below), because both conditions may respond.

Dopamine-Blocking Agents

Should an alpha agonist provide insufficient benefit, we generally add or replace it with a dopamine receptor blocker. These are the most potent and predictably effective tic-suppressing medications. Classical neuroleptic antipsychotics, including haloperidol, pimozide, and fluphenazine, have documented efficacy in controlled clinical trials. These drugs fell out of favor because of frequent side effects, especially sedation, depression and mental dulling, and the introduction of the newer atypical antipsychotics. Although we tend to use an atypical antipsychotic (usually risperidone or aripiprazole) as our initial dopamine-blocking agent, they are often poorly tolerated because of sedation, weight gain, and development of the metabolic syndrome (abdominal obesity, dyslipidemia, hypertension, and impaired glucose metabolism). The pendulum may be swinging back to more frequent use of classical antipsychotics, which also tend to be less expensive. Not all atypical antipsychotics have equivalent tic-suppressing effects. Risperidone and olanzapine showed efficacy in randomized controlled trials, whereas clozapine and quetiapine seem to be less effective for tics. Initial reports (and our own experience) in the use of the mixed dopamine agonist/antagonist aripiprazole have shown benefit for tics, but no controlled trials have yet been published. It should be noted that tardive dyskinesia, a feared side effect of dopamine-blocking drugs, seems to be a rare occurrence in treated TS patients, possibly due to their underlying state of altered dopamine neurotransmission. We usually prescribe a dopamine blocker in a single bedtime dose, but the dosage can be divided if needed.

Other Tic-Suppressing Drugs

Although the usual medication treatment for tics centers on alpha agonists and antipsychotics, other types of drugs may be of benefit for patients having an inadequate response or problems with tolerability. Clonazepam has had reported modest tic-suppressing effects in published case series. This drug may be particularly useful in patients with an associated anxiety disorder. It is usually given two or three times daily, and its most common side effects are sedation and unsteadiness. The dopamine-depleting drug tetrabenazine has possible efficacy. The drug is marketed in Canada and Europe and is expected to become available soon in the United States. In an open-label study the

Among children with TS, males are affected three times more often than females.

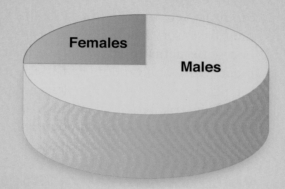

Taken from: "Facts About Tourette Syndrome," Centers for Disease Control and Prevention, September 6, 2011. www.cdc.gov.

drug showed sustained moderate to marked reduction in tics over an average of 2 years' follow-up. However, only 22% of subjects were free of side effects. The most common side effects are sedation, depression, insomnia, and parkinsonism [a neurological disorder similar to Parkinson's disease]. Children may tolerate higher doses of tetrabenazine than adults. In both age groups, the drug is usually given in two or three daily doses. Although tetrabenazine does not cause tardive [belated] phenomena, dopamine-depleting agents can cause neuroleptic malignant syndrome even after years of use.

Local injections of botulinum toxin can be considered when one or a few tics within the patient's repertoire are a significant source of social distress, discomfort, or self-injury. When tics have dystonic features, such as holding of a sustained neck posture or sustained eye closure, botulinum toxin may be a preferred treatment. Dramatic improvements in pain or near-blindness from such tics has been reported. Similar benefit has been reported for cervical tics associated with myelopathy or laryngeal injections for severe vocal tics including coprolalia. Many patients treated with botulinum toxin report a lessening or disappearance of their urges to tic or in their premonitory sensations in the sites injected. Botulinum may modify sensory feedback (such as from intrafusal muscle fibers) perpetuating processes involved in tic reinforcement. Only one randomized trial with botulinum toxin for tics has been reported. Two weeks after injection, a significant reduction in number of motor tics was observed. The most common side effects of botulinum toxin injections are weakness and pain. . . .

Potential Alternative Drugs

Anecdotal reports from TS patients that marijuana use ameliorates their tics may have scientific relevance given evidence that basal ganglia cannabinoid receptors modulate dopamine, glutamate, and GABA [gamma-aminobutyric acid] activity governing motoric output. Delta-9-tetrahydrocannabinol has shown promise for efficacy in a small placebo-controlled crossover study. Further studies using drugs acting on cannabinoid receptors, such as dronabinol or nabilone, may be rational.

Given the 4:1 male to female predominance in TS and the typical peak of symptoms around puberty, a role for androgens has been proposed. Mild tic reduction was reported for the androgen blocker flutamide in a placebo-controlled crossover trial. Finasteride had dramatic benefit reported for one case of neuroleptic-refractory TS with comorbid self-injurious tics and compulsions.

Behavioral Therapy Can Help Control Tourette Syndrome

Jeannine Stein

Tourette syndrome (TS) patients can benefit from a specialized kind of behavioral therapy, reports Jeannine Stein in the following selection. According to a study conducted at the University of California–Los Angeles, ten weeks of a tic-reducing behavioral therapy resulted in significant improvement in 53 percent of the participants. The main component of this therapy is habit reversal training, which teaches a patient to channel his or her urge to tic into a less noticeable voluntary behavior, the author explains. While the therapy is not a cure for TS, it teaches patients an effective, nonmedical way to manage their tics, allowing them to take a more active role in their treatment. Stein is a health writer for the *Los Angeles Times*.

Tourette syndrome—a neurological disorder characterized by involuntary tics such as blinking, head-jerking and loud sounds—can be devastating for children, setting them up for teasing and ostracism, while the drugs used to treat the condition have

SOURCE: Jeannine Stein, "Behavioral Therapy Effective in Treating Tourette Syndrome," *Los Angeles Times*, May 18, 2010. All rights reserved. Reproduced by permission.

significant side effects. Now a study has found that behavioral therapy may help lessen tics in children and teens about as effectively as medication.

In the study, released Tuesday [May 18, 2010] in the *Journal of the American Medical Assn.*, 126 children ages 9 to 17 who had Tourette or a chronic tic disorder were randomly assigned to 10 weeks of behavioral therapy designed to reduce the tics, or to a control group that received support therapy and education. About a third of all children were also on anti-tic medication. The study treatment included a functional intervention to better manage anxiety-producing social situations.

Some participants in the therapy group received "booster" treatments at three and six months after the 10-week therapy sessions.

> **FAST FACT**
>
> A 2010 Yale University study of children with TS found that 52.5 percent experienced significant improvement after undergoing a form of cognitive behavioral therapy.

Improvement in More than Half the Cases

At the end of the study, about 53% of the children in the therapy group were judged significantly improved, compared with 19% of the children in the control group. Tics worsened in one child in the therapy group and in four in the control group.

At six months, 87% of the children who completed therapy and had not dropped out of the study still showed benefits from the therapy.

The therapy group's results were about the same as recent studies examining the effectiveness of medication, the study's authors said. These drugs include antidepressants and anti-anxiety medications as well as antipsychotics such as risperidone and haloperidol. Some have side effects such as weight gain, lethargy and anxiety.

Habit Reversal Training

The therapy, called comprehensive behavioral intervention for tics, has several elements. The key component, habit reversal training, helps patients become more aware of the urge to tic, then teaches them to engage in a voluntary behavior—rhythmic breathing, perhaps—that competes with the tic. Though the therapy doesn't suppress the urge to tic, it channels the urge into another, less noticeable behavior.

Habit reversal training has been used for decades to treat disorders such as trichotillomania (compulsive hair pulling or twisting), and compulsive nail biting and skin picking. Its use for treating Tourette syndrome has become more widespread in the last 10 years.

"We don't look at the treatment as a cure for Tourette," said John Piacentini, lead author of the study and a professor of psychiatry and biobehavioral sciences at UCLA [University of California–Los Angeles]. "We're teaching the child an effective means of managing their tics—and in the best cases, they can learn to manage them until the tics do gradually disappear. More realistically, they can

A young boy diagnosed with Tourette syndrome and his mother work with a psychologist on behavioral therapy. (© Ted Richardson/MCT/ Landov)

manage them so they don't happen with such frequency that they significantly interfere with the child's life."

Making the Patient an Active Agent

Although habit reversal training has gained more acceptance in recent years, Piacentini says that some critics have seen the therapy as simply replacing one tic with another.

But Peter Hollenbeck, professor of biological sciences at Purdue University and chairman of the Tourette Syndrome Assn.'s scientific advisory board, said the behavioral treatment puts the control in the hands of the person with Tourette.

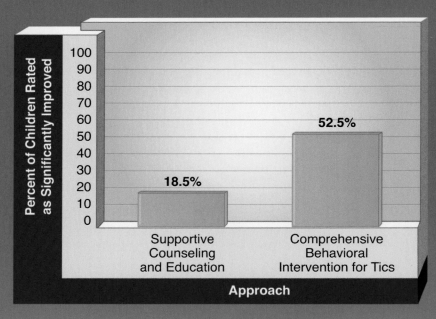

A Comparison of Two Approaches to Treating Tourette Syndrome: The Yale Study

Taken from: "Children Can Be Taught to Manage Tourette Syndrome Tics." *Yale News*, May 18, 2010. www.news.yale.edu.

"As opposed to saying, 'Sit back and take your [medication] and hope for the best,' this is a set of skills to learn," he said. "This puts you in the position of being an active agent."

Piacentini, who is director of UCLA's Childhood OCD, Anxiety & Tic Disorders Program, said more work needed to be done to understand why a sizable number of children did not benefit from the therapy.

"We're looking at the data to see if we can identify which factors were associated with the best response," he said. "Maybe we need to revise the therapy, or combine it with therapies or medication."

The researchers are also studying brain imaging before and after the therapy to see how the therapy may change the brain.

"Medicine may play an important role in treatment," Piacentini added. "But it makes the most sense to start with behavioral treatment, since it's safe and effective in many cases."

Identifying and Minimizing Environmental Triggers Can Help Control Tourette Syndrome

Sheila Rogers

Tourette syndrome (TS) is frequently aggravated by certain foods, chemicals, and physical or environmental factors, argues Sheila Rogers in the following viewpoint. While TS is a genetic condition, research suggests that it is also an environmental condition. Rogers rejects the common explanation that tic symptoms naturally wax and wane; she contends that an increase in tics is caused by a change within the body as it reacts to an environmental stimulus. Rogers encourages TS patients and their families to observe closely and keep records so that they can discover what triggers an increase in tics. The author is the director of the Association for Comprehensive NeuroTherapy, a nonprofit organization dedicated to exploring alternative treatments for Tourette syndrome, obsessive-compulsive disorder, attention-deficit/hyperactivity disorder, and related conditions.

A parent contacted the Association for Comprehensive NeuroTherapy (ACN) to report: We have learned that our son's Tourette syndrome (TS) symptoms can be triggered by environmental stimuli. For example, milk causes a "Mmm-mm" vocal sound in Don. A trip to an amusement park that included a ride on a diesel-powered bumper car resulted in tics that were far worse than any he'd had before. . . . We went out of town for a week, during which time he was tic-free. Within minutes of returning to our home, which had been closed up with a strong air freshener, tics began. We have noticed that tics often worsen after mealtime. Pollens seem to increase tics. Smoke from a forest fire caused a neck twitch that lasted one day. . . .

Many people with Tourette syndrome (TS) report that certain foods, toxic chemicals, or other environmental situations make their tics worse. But how can this be if TS is a "genetic" condition? Research confirms that Tourette syndrome (TS) is a genetic—and an environmental—condition.

What does this mean? Just think of allergies. Someone can have a genetic predisposition to develop allergic reactions, but, as everyone knows, the environment can greatly determine the types and intensity of symptoms he or she will experience. In a similar manner, many people with TS report they are aware of certain triggers for their tics that affect the frequency, type, or severity of the tics.

It is generally accepted that stress, excitement, and fatigue can aggravate tics. But numerous other factors may also prove to be involved, and the more aware a person with TS is about potential triggers, the more likely he or she can identify them. In general, environmental factors include what we eat, see, hear, breathe, drink, touch, smell, and otherwise come in contact with. They can encompass natal and prenatal conditions, temperature and lighting, stress, emotions, and fatigue, as well as vaccines, medications, viruses, and bacterial infections.

Defining Environmental Triggers

For the past few years, the Association for Comprehensive NeuroTherapy (ACN) has been collecting information on what aggravates tics, with information coming from patients, families, and health care professionals. The responses have come through questionnaires, feedback at conferences, personally questioning physicians, and by gleaning information from letters received.

A review of hundreds of responses suggests a set of rather common stimuli, with numerous less frequent ones. Those less frequently reported may indeed be less responsible for aggravating tics—or they may simply be more difficult to recognize and/or less often considered.

The list we are providing includes relatively immediate exposures/foods for vocal and/or motor tics, in contrast to factors like vaccines or exposure to a toxin years before the onset of TS. Each item listed can have an impact on the central nervous system of some people with Tourette syndrome, but what is troublesome to one person may not bother another. I hope the discussion that follows and this preliminary list will empower families and patients to begin collecting their own information on triggers. I also hope it will encourage physicians and researchers to consider collecting and sharing similar information.

The Waxing and Waning of Symptoms

When someone asks a doctor why tics can be worse on one day than another or why they may disappear for weeks, months, or even years at a time, they are usually told that this is what tics do—it is a *characteristic* of TS: symptoms wax—and then they wane. Unfortunately, this circular reasoning doesn't answer the question.

Tics come and go because something within the body is changing. The tics are symptoms of that change. How many physicians empower patients to actively try to solve this puzzle, to find the cause of increased tic frequency or

A Preliminary List of Triggers

Most Common (in alphabetical order)

Alcohol
Artificial colors and flavors
Cleaning chemicals
Caffeine
Dairy
Dust
Excitement
Infections (bacterial/viral)
Molds
Perfumes/scented products
Pollens
Preservatives/MSG
Stimulant medication
Stress
Sweets/sodas/cane sugar

Reported, but Less Frequently (and not necessarily less troublesome)

Artificial sweeteners
Carpeting (new)
Carpeting (removal)
Cell phone use
Chicken pox
Chlorine
Clothing/fabric sensation on skin
Corn
Dental related causes (spacers, losing teeth)
Dry cleaning odors
Fabric softener
Feeling hungry
Foods—numerous; most common ones listed
Formaldehyde
Fumes from fuel
Heat (temperature increase)
Hepatitis B Vaccine
Lawn treatment
Light (flashing, bright, or fluorescent)
Medications (antihistamines, decongestants)
Nitrates/processed meats
Noise
Orange juice
Paint and thinners
Pesticides
Smoke
Television
Wheat
Yeasty foods
Video games

Taken from: Sheila Rogers. "Finding Triggers for Tics." *Latitudes*, 2007.

severity? How many suggest that people try to understand the conditions existing when the tics have subsided—what might have changed that allowed this tic-free or tic-reduced period? The answer, of course, is very few. Instead, most parents and patients feel powerless, and they usually accept the condition as a genetic medical problem over which they can have little influence.

1. *Not everyone may be able to identify triggers for their TS.* ACN presumes that there are different subsets of TS; it is easier to recognize what aggravates symptoms in some people than in others. We do not know what percentage of those with TS experience at least one food or exposure that bothers them, though we predict that it is a majority.

2. *The knowledge is not yet available to detect all possible factors* that may be affecting tics. Consider what happens when someone has an outbreak of hives. While hives are recognized as an immune response to some environmental factor, in a majority of cases their actual cause goes undetected, even with careful investigation and professional assistance. Finding triggers for TS can be more complex than tracking down the source of a case of hives. Sometimes there are so many tics that it is extremely difficult to separate one potential cause from another. Or the cause could be so subtle—like a low-grade chronic infection—that it isn't even considered.

3. *It is possible to be mistaken.* One might blame an observable increase in tics on "dairy" because a flare-up in symptoms regularly occurs after eating ice cream. Yet it could actually be the artificial flavors, corn syrup, or chocolate chips in the ice cream that were to blame—or it could be that all of these items are culprits, including the dairy.

4. *Repeat observation brings the best results.* Assuming a connection between a single-incident stimulus and an increase in tics can be misleading. So many factors can potentially be involved that it often requires record-keeping and repeat occurrences to be sure.

Why Bother Looking for Triggers?

The purpose of identifying environmental insults that aggravate tics is, of course, so they can be avoided whenever possible. The list of potential triggers for tics is extensive. ACN suggests you commit to making a serious effort for six weeks or more to see if you can find a connection between tics and aggravating environmental factors. With each discovery, you should feel more empowered.

Will you find all the answers you need? That's impossible to say. But given that TS can be a lifelong condition, you can at least decide to make an effort. It would be a shame to look back in fifteen years and say, "I had no idea the food I was giving my child for breakfast was making the tics worse." Unfortunately, we've heard many such comments.

> **FAST FACT**
>
> A study conducted by Thomas Verstraeten of the Centers for Disease Control and Prevention in 2003 suggests that exposure to thimerosal, an ingredient used in some vaccines, can cause tics.

We Are All Biologically Different

Wouldn't it be great if all cases of TS were identical? Everyone could take one prescription medication that would act in precisely the same manner for each person. Yet we know this is far from the case. Finding a suitable drug to treat TS usually involves experimentation—trying one drug for a short time, adjusting dosage, then switching or adding different meds in an attempt to achieve tolerable side effects and long-lasting results.

Why is there not a one-size-fits-all medication for TS? *Because people are biologically different.* Please remember this when you review the list . . . . Don't give up after exploring just a few items listed as common ones, and don't be surprised if you find new ones not on the list. Don't limit your investigation solely based on other people's findings.

What is remarkable about trigger identification for TS to date is that patients and families have mostly discovered aggravating factors on their own. They have usually done

Certain foods, such as ice cream, are environmental triggers that may cause an increase in tics in Tourette syndrome sufferers. (© Lisa Barber/Alamy)

this without the support, guidance, or suggestions of their regular medical practitioner. In fact, their exploration is often met with discouraging remarks or resistance. Each person who has shared with ACN on this topic should be commended for thinking outside the box and for taking the time to help others.

The environmental factors listed . . . are informally grouped according to the rate at which they have been reported to ACN. There is no connection between how common a trigger may be and its impact or severity. As an example, exposure to chlorine, which was not highly reported, could potentially cause a more significant reaction than caffeine, depending on individual sensitivities.

Where Should Families Start?

Keep a log. Make notes on the occurrence or state of tics at regular times during the day, such as upon awakening, after breakfast, at lunch (when possible), after school or sports, etc., and before bed. Use a recording method that is comfortable for you. Note what might have been responsible for an increase or decrease in tics, such as foods eaten, a special activity, a particular location, a new shampoo, renovations in the home, or lawn treatment. If you're a relative of a child with TS, in addition to your own observations, you can ask what he or she thinks may have caused a reaction and try to spark an awareness of the situation.

Sometimes people feel so frustrated with the process of watching for triggers that they throw up their hands and quit. Our advice is this: if you have ever observed any situation or stimulus that you know resulted in tics getting worse, you at least know that the cause and effect connection is real. You know factors beyond genetics are within your understanding and, hopefully, within your control. Be patient and thorough as you begin to explore other possibilities.

Let's say you have a son, and his tics seem worse after a baseball game. Was it the stress of the game? The Gatorade the coach passed out? Fatigue from playing? Summer heat? Pesticides sprayed on the field before the game? It takes detective work, and it's not always easy. Don't expect to find your answers all at once.

ACN recognizes that most people are already stressed, that they are already emotionally or otherwise consumed just from dealing with the condition of TS, not to mention life's universal daily stressors. But if connections are found between tics and environmental stimuli, it can be a life-altering experience. Keep noting the intensity, frequency, and types of tics, as well as possible related factors. Watch for a pattern. . . .

Taking Action

Once aggravating factors are identified, the next step is to determine what you're going to do about them. Parents frequently contact us and say, for example, that they know "x, y, or z" increases their child's tics—but, they add, how could they ever withhold these items or situations from their youngster?

Parents should understand that a child with TS has an illness. His or her nervous system is hypersensitive or hyper-excitable, and it needs to be thought of in these terms. If indeed something is making the symptoms worse—something that can be controlled—then it's important that you, as the parent, do your best to help the child avoid those items. Adults with TS can make these decisions for themselves. Just as many adults decide that they prefer living with their tics to enduring the side effects of certain medications, they may also decide to continue indulging in a particular habit they know aggravates their tics. That is their decision. But a child should be provided with the most wholesome environment possible, and this is naturally the responsibility of the parents. Other preventive and medical approaches can be pursued to strengthen the immune and nervous systems in an effort to reduce the level of sensitivity to the environment.

ACN hears frequently that someone was able to identify at least one trigger for tics, and when they told a physician or psychologist, the response was, "That's ridiculous," or "It's a coincidence," or "You're wasting your time" in these pursuits.

This is medicine at its worst. After all, TS is referred to in the literature as a "mystery." There is no lab result to verify its existence. The best specialists in the world do not have all the answers. Yet patients and families are coming to professionals around the world and offering clues to help solve this mystery. More frequently than not, they encounter a deaf ear and may even be discouraged from further exploration.

Dietary Changes Can Help Control Tourette Syndrome

Bruce Semon

Bruce Semon is a child, adolescent, and adult psychiatrist who has extensively studied nutrition and homeopathy. Stationed in Glendale, Wisconsin, Semon is the medical director of the Wisconsin Institute of Nutrition and the coauthor of *Feast Without Yeast: 4 Stages to Better Health*. In the following selection Semon discusses the case of a boy with Tourette syndrome (TS) who consulted him after experiencing bad side effects from medicines conventionally used to control tics. Semon placed the boy on an anti-yeast diet and prescribed a yeast-killing medicine for him. Within a few months the boy experienced a great reduction in tics and lost the weight he had gained with his previous medications.

With TS the inhibitory function of the brain is impaired, the author points out. Yeast creates sedative chemicals that slow the brain down; in a TS patient, yeast causes a suppression of the brain's natural inhibitory functions and an increase in tics. Excluding yeast from the diet greatly benefits people with this disorder, Semon concludes.

Don came to me at the age of 11 to get help with Tourette's and the side effects of medications. He had had Tourette's symptoms for four years and had been diagnosed five months previously. At that time, the tics had suddenly become worse with coprolalia (involuntary utterance of obscene words). His coprolalia was so bad that he was saying four letter words continuously from the time he got out of bed. Before that he had only facial tics.

His neurological examination was normal except for the tics. A number of anti-psychotic medications were tried. Orap was tried for six weeks, but he gained twenty pounds. Then Risperdal (an anti-psychotic) was tried but he had nausea and increased breast tissue. He lasted two months on Risperdal. Then Zyprexa (an anti-psychotic) was tried which controlled the tics but he had scenes of visual rage. Paxil (an anti-depressant) was added. The visual scenes decreased and were now intermittent. He was now fatigued, sleeping a lot and was hard to rouse in the morning. He had mood swings. When he was down or frustrated, his moods were extreme. He had gained twenty more pounds with the Zyprexa. Vitamins had been tried with no benefit but craniosacral therapy had helped with mood swings. He had a history of using antibiotics in the past.

Before the worsening of the tics, he was not moody. He was popular and was voted to student council. He was outgoing and was a smart kid. Now he was moody. He also had a symptom of obsessive compulsive disorder (a disorder in which people either think something or must do something over and over): that he needed to confess things, and he had to come to [his] mother for this.

The Anti-Yeast Strategy

By the time I saw this patient his tics were under better control. He displayed no coprolalia at the first visit. When he was first seen he was taking Zyprexa and Paxil (an anti-depressant). He was having vocal and motor tics when seen and he had some thoughts of suicide. He was overweight and was seeing visual scenes of rage. He was 50 pounds overweight.

He started the anti-yeast diet and nystatin. When he came back four weeks later, his moods had leveled out, he had gotten off both his medications, and he had lost three pounds. He had more facial tics but other tics had not returned. He had had some nausea in trying to get off Paxil, but this was better now. He was still obsessive about confessing guilt. Sleep was alright. He was taking nystatin ¼ tsp. four times a day. On exam his mood was pleasant and he was laughing and smiling. He was blinking his eyes and moving some facial muscles and was moving his head a little. Neurological exam was normal except for the tics.

> **FAST FACT**
>
> Tardive dyskinesia, a neurological condition that causes uncontrollable mouth movements and drooling, is a serious side-effect of some tic-suppressing drugs.

At this time he was off the medications, on the anti-yeast diet and nystatin, and had actually fewer tics now than while on the meds. I suggested that the treatment be continued. He came back at three months after the first visit and he was still following the diet except for eating a little chocolate on Sundays as a reward. His tics had increased a little with some coprolalia and some motor tics. Emotionally he was doing very well. He had lost about five pounds. He was confessing less often and to fewer things. He was sleeping reasonably well. On exam a few vocal tics were heard. He swung his arms occasionally and he was smiling.

A Great Reduction in Tics

He came back at six months after starting treatment and he said that he was doing fine in school (a Sept. appt.) He was doing well in football. He was keeping up with the other kids much better than last year, and he was getting along with his classmates. The teachers said that things were fine. He was still blinking his eyes and making a few vocal sounds. The force of his verbal tics had decreased, although his tics were worse with stress and varied from day to day. One teacher who had not known him previously had not noticed anything unusual. He was no longer apologizing for everything. On exam a few eyeblinks were noted. He was much thinner. No vocal tics were heard.

His parents sent me a Christmas card with the patient smiling in his football uniform.

At the next visit, a year after first being seen, his mother estimated his motor tics were down about 95% and his vocal tics are down 98%. He is no longer confessing to things. He has lost the weight he gained with the medications. At the appointment, some eyeblinking was observed but no other tics. He is on no psychiatric medications and the few tics he has are not interfering with his life.

Three months later, at his most recent visit, his mother reported that the vocal tics are gone and there are only occasional motor tics.

Tourette Syndrome and Yeast

Motor tics are repetitive motions of muscles which are only partially under voluntary control and may range from eye blinking to complicated motions of the trunk and arms. Vocal tics are the involuntary repetitive saying of words or short phrases, which can unfortunately include swear words. When both of these occur in the same person, the disorder is called Tourette's disorder. There is no known cure and the medicines used are "heavies" (anti-psychotic medicines which have many side effects).

I have treated several cases of Tourette's successfully using anti-yeast therapy and nystatin. This treatment clears out intestinal yeast. The yeast is making chemicals which slow the brain down. Why might this therapy be helpful? I offer the following thoughts.

Foods Allowed on a Yeast-Free Diet

- Vegetables
- Beans
- Meat protein: beef, poultry, fish, uncured pork
- Eggs
- Whole grains: rice, oats, barley, millet, buckwheat
- Pasta made of corn, rice, or spelt
- Unprocessed seeds and nuts
- Unrefined vegetable oils

For a tic to occur, a center in the brain must fire, triggering the muscles to move. In normal individuals, such centers do not fire involuntarily. The reason that these centers do not fire involuntarily is that most of the brain is devoted to keeping the brain centers ready to work but not actually working. The brain allows the part we want to be active to focus on what we want. For example, if I wish to reach out and pick something off a table, my arm and hand move to pick it up. This motion does not take my whole brain to do. The rest of my brain is making sure that I focus only on what I want to do. At the same time, the brain is making sure that, for example, my legs do not move when I reach out with my arm. The majority of the brain is inhibitory; that is, it keeps most of the brain ready but not actually working unless that part of the brain is needed.

In Tourette's the inhibitory function is decreased, so a brain center, instead of being told to wait until needed, can simply fire and do what it does, such as blink an eye.

The author claims that dietary changes, such as the elimination of yeast, can result in a reduction of tics in Tourette syndrome patients. (© Steve Stock/Alamy)

The problem is partially that a center is too active, but it is also that the rest of the brain is not working properly. The rest of the brain should be inhibiting this overactive center but does not.

Toxic Sedative Chemicals

We can understand how this might be the case if there are toxic sedative chemicals slowing the brain down. The parts of the brain which keep other centers ready but not actually working are themselves slowed down. Then if another center wishes to fire, it is not being inhibited and it fires.

Where are these toxic sedative chemicals coming from? The intestinal yeast *Candida* produces a number of toxic alcohols and the coma producing chemical acetone.

Sedative chemicals also are found in food. For example vinegar contains a chemical, ethyl acetate, which is a sedative. Malt contain chemicals called pyrazines, which sedate and slow the brain down.

The clinical observations are that when the toxic sedative chemicals are removed, then the rest of the brain does its function of inhibition. Then these active centers also function only when they are supposed to. Then Tourette's symptoms diminish considerably.

An Effective Treatment

This understanding leads to a safe effective treatment for Tourette's disorder. This treatment is simply to clear out the intestinal *Candida* and to stop eating foods with sedative chemicals. Then the yeast will stop making sedative chemicals. Then the brain will no longer be slowed down, will work better and will inhibit active centers from firing.

The treatment consists of taking a non-absorbed medicine called nystatin. Nystatin kills intestinal yeast. The problem is that nystatin does not work well without changes of food choices. The reason is that in many foods there are chemicals which kill bacteria and feed the yeast. If these foods are left in the diet, even though nystatin kills the yeast, the yeast will keep growing back. Chemicals in the diet which kill bacteria will make room for the yeast, even if nystatin is taken. When foods containing these chemicals are excluded from the diet, then nystatin can go through and kill the yeast and the yeast does not grow back. Then problems such as Tourette's disorder improve significantly. These same foods contain the toxic sedative chemicals.

The diet for *Candida* problems consists of removing fermented foods from the diet. The worst offenders are alcoholic beverages and non-alcoholic beer, vinegar, barley malt, chocolate, pickles, and aged cheese. I explain the diet very thoroughly, including how to implement the diet for children, in *An Extraordinary Power to Heal* and *Feast Without Yeast: 4 Stages to Better Health.*

Self-Hypnosis Can Help Control Tourette Syndrome

University Hospitals Case Medical Center

The following piece is drawn from a study conducted by physicians Jeffrey Lazarus and Susan K. Klein of the University Hospitals Case Medical Center in Cleveland, Ohio. This study focused on thirty-three young Tourette syndrome patients who were taught self-hypnosis, a practice that facilitates a mental state that combines relaxation with concentration on a particular goal. When the patients had reached this highly focused state, they were given suggestions on how to control their tics. The researchers found that nearly all the participants experienced greatly increased tic control after only a few sessions of guided self-hypnosis. This technique could serve as an alternative to medications, particularly for children with mild or moderate tic disorders.

A new study of children and adolescents with Tourette Syndrome finds that self-hypnosis taught with the aid of videotape training reduced their symptoms and improved their quality of life.

SOURCE: "Children and Teens with Tourette Syndrome Find Relief with Self-Hypnosis," *Science Daily*, July 12, 2010. Based on news release issued by University Hospitals Case Medical Center. All rights reserved. Reproduced by permission.

Seventy-nine percent of the 33 research participants achieved enough improvement in tic control to report personal satisfaction with the technique, according to the study published online in the July [2010] issue of the *Journal of Development and Behavioral Pediatrics*. This is the largest case series of patients with Tourette Syndrome treated with self-hypnosis. The authors, Jeffrey Lazarus, M.D., and Susan K. Klein, M.D., Ph.D., were with University Hospitals Rainbow Babies & Children's Hospital and the Case Western Reserve University School of Medicine at the time of the study.

A study of children and adolescents with Tourette syndrome found that self-hypnosis reduced their symptoms and improved their quality of life. (© **Bubbles Photolibrary/Alamy**)

The Nature of the Study

Subjects were shown video clips of a young boy with Tourette Syndrome before, during, and after his self-hypnosis training. Following that, each child or teen in the study was taught self-hypnosis in individual sessions. The participants ranged in age from 6 to 19 years, with an average of 13 years.

The research subjects also were assigned to practice the self-hypnosis technique three times a day and homework to answer questions designed to increase their awareness of tics and how they felt about experiencing them. All of the research participants had motor tics and three had verbal tics in their initial evaluations.

According to Dr. Lazarus, self-hypnosis helps the patient experience a state of mind that combines relaxation with concentration on a desired point of focus while other thoughts or feelings fade into the background.

> **FAST FACT**
>
> The word *hypnosis* is derived from Scottish physician James Braid's term *neuro-hynosis,* meaning "sleep of the nervous system."

"Once the patient is in his or her highly focused 'special place,' work is then done on controlling the tic," said Dr. Lazarus. "We ask the patient to imagine the feeling right before that tic occurs and to put up a stop sign in front of it, or to imagine a tic switch that can be turned on and off like a light switch. Further suggestions are made, including encouraging the patient to invent his or her own images."

Almost all of the participants experienced a dramatic increase in tic control after only a few sessions: 12 after two sessions, 13 after only three visits, and one after four visits.

An Alternative to Medications

Dr. Lazarus says that this non-pharmacological therapy for tics is attractive because the medications that are used to treat tics can be associated with undesirable side effects. Also, physicians are reluctant to prescribe medi-

Side Effects of Tic–Suppressing Medications

Side Effect	Clonidine	Risperidone	Haloperidol	Aripiprazole	Clonazepam
Constipation	✓	✓	✓		
Dizziness	✓	✓	✓	✓	✓
Tiredness	✓	✓			
Headache	✓	✓			
Insomnia	✓	✓			✓
Anxiety		✓			
Nausea/vomiting		✓	✓		✓
Loss of coordination					✓
High blood sugar				✓	
High blood pressure				✓	
Weight gain		✓		✓	
Suicidal thoughts				✓	

Taken from: www.drugs.com, 2012.

cations for mild or moderate tic disorders, which many children often outgrow as they get older.

"This case series suggests that self-hypnosis might be able to be taught effectively in fewer sessions than another technique known as habit reversal, but we'll need to study this further. However, the use of videotape as a teaching aid presents several advantages: It can help standardize the technique of teaching the method, it may shorten the length of time needed to teach the technique, and it makes the technique more accessible to younger children. Viewing a series of videotapes of another patient gives patients the reassurance that they are not the only ones in the world with this problem, and it gives them hope and the motivation that they can take control of their bodies and life challenges," said Dr. Lazarus.

A Combination of Therapies Can Help Control Tourette Syndrome

Robert A. King and James F. Leckman

Robert A. King is a professor of child psychiatry and the medical direc-tor of the Tourette's/Obsessive-Compulsive Disorder Clinic at the Yale School of Medicine. James F. Leckman is a professor of pediatrics and psychiatry at the Yale School of Medicine. The following selec-tion is excerpted from a blog in the *New York Times* in which these physicians answer readers' questions about Tourette syndrome (TS). Each question addresses a different situation. In their responses, the doctors explain how combinations of various medications—as well as psychotherapy and experimental treatments—can provide relief from the debilitating symptoms of TS and related conditions such as obsessive-compulsive disorder.

M.S. from Boston asks: I am the mother of two sons, 13 and 16. My husband struggled with O.C.D. (obsessive-compulsive disorder) most of his early adulthood and has been on medications for 20 years; he is mostly symptom free. My 16-year-old son was diagnosed with O.C.D. at 7 and has done CBT [cognitive-behavioral therapy] and has been on Prozac for many years. He is mostly symptom free.

My 13-year-old son, whom I consider to be very anxious, is starting to look Tourette's-like to me. He often says very nasty things to me and other family members, and immediately follows with "I'm sorry, I didn't mean to say that." He also displays tic-like behavior, sort of spastic facial movements and such. What should I do?

Dr. King and Dr. Leckman respond: Tics and obsessive-compulsive disorder often occur together, and the coming *Diagnostic and Statistical Manual of Mental Disorders*, the DSM-V, which health care professionals use to identify specific mental health diagnoses, will very likely have an entry on "tic-related O.C.D."

The good news is that tic disorders and tic-related O.C.D. will often ease, or even disappear, by early adulthood. The bad news is that sometimes you need to use higher doses of SSRI [selective serotonin reuptake inhibitor] antidepressant medications, like Prozac, to get a beneficial response. In addition, at times it is necessary to augment the SSRI with another medication. In a recent study, we also found that many of our "remitted" O.C.D. cases continued to take an SSRI.

The best treatment for early onset, tic-related O.C.D. is usually a combination of medication and CBT (cognitive-behavioral therapy), often a specific technique called exposure and response prevention. It sounds like this combination has been beneficial for your 16-year-old.

Exposure and Response Prevention

With exposure and response prevention, the patient and therapist develop a ladder or hierarchy of worries along with corresponding rituals or compulsions. This hierarchy runs from least worrisome and compelling to most worrisome and compelling.

During a therapeutic session, the patient and therapist begin with some mutually agreed upon symptom.

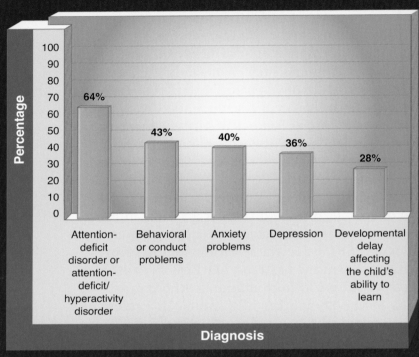

Prevalence of Selected Diagnoses Among People Aged 6–17 Years Who Have Ever Received a Diagnosis of TS

Percentage

64%

43%

40%

36%

28%

Attention-deficit disorder or attention-deficit/hyperactivity disorder

Behavioral or conduct problems

Anxiety problems

Depression

Developmental delay affecting the child's ability to learn

Diagnosis

Taken from: By parent report, National Survey of Children's Health, United States, 2007.

The patient, with the therapist's help, then deliberately exposes himself to a feared, but manageable, situation and then refrains for an agreed upon period of time from doing the compulsion that he usually does to neutralize the worry.

For example, someone with a contamination/germ/washing form of O.C.D. might touch an object they regard as moderately contaminated, like the rug, and then refrain from immediately washing or using a hand sanitizer. Together with the therapist, the patient rates and tracks the level of anxiety involved and charts it every few minutes. The patient learns that if the worry isn't immediately "short-circuited" by doing the ritual, in this case washing, the anxiety gradually diminishes over the course of the session. One of the things that keeps O.C.D. going is that in the short run, it is easiest to give in and do the compulsion or to avoid the feared situation; this provides short-term relief, but at the cost of ever more extensive rituals or avoidance. Homework consists of planning and practicing such exposures between sessions.

Without knowing the details of your 13-year-old's situation, we would add that one of the challenges of parenting a youngster with a tic disorder is learning to distinguish—and helping your child distinguish—between true tics and general teenage impulsive behavior. True tics would include complex vocal tics—for example, saying something nasty when one has no intention of doing so, and when what is said is not at all congruent with how one is feeling at the moment. Impulsive behavior, which is easier to keep under voluntary control, might include a young teen's irritable lashing out at a parent with whom they are momentarily annoyed.

This isn't always an easy distinction to make. It is important, on the one hand, to avoid stigmatizing or punishing a child for something that he or she really cannot control. On the other hand, it's also important to help a child control what he or she may be able to. Consultation with a clinician knowledgeable about tic disorders and O.C.D. may be helpful in sorting this out.

When Tics Worsen Later in Life

kronos5 from N.J. asks: I have had the symptoms of Tourette's since I was 4 years old. Now, at 54, I find these symptoms have not abated. In fact, they are in many ways worse than ever. Within the last five years or so, I have also started to vocalize, which I did not do before. I thought I would be over this by now.

Is this a normal course for Tourette's syndrome? I was never bothered by the social interaction aspects of this before, but now they are starting to trouble me. What would be my best course of action? I have never tried medication. Should I consider it?

Dr. King and Dr. Leckman respond: The symptoms of Tourette's syndrome very often settle down in early adulthood, and it is unusual for the vocal tics to appear at your age. When we encounter a story like yours, we will often be on the lookout for stressful life events or the emergence of a medical problem like an overactive thyroid.

Medications may be of some help, and you should consult with a physician knowledgeable about the treatment of Tourette's. For many people, medications can be helpful for tics as well as coexisting conditions like obsessive-compulsive disorder or attention-deficit hyperactivity disorder, or A.D.H.D.

For tics, the best evidence supports the use of drugs called neuroleptics, like risperidone (Risperdal) or aripiprazole (Abilify), that most likely affect levels of the brain chemical dopamine. Other classes of medications, like the so-called alpha agonists, like guanfacine or clonidine, are also sometimes used, but the evidence is weaker for these drugs. But well-controlled studies with these agents show they can be quite helpful for some people, particularly those with coexisting attention and hyperactivity problems.

In other cases, medications that were initially developed to help patients with seizure disorders have been helpful for people with Tourette's. Periodic injections of botulinum toxin, or Botox, into specific muscle groups can also be helpful for localized tics. But truth be told, we still do not have ideal anti-tic medications that are effective and work in the short term without many side effects.

FAST FACT

Most TS patients experience their worst symptoms in their early teens, with improvement occurring in the late teens and adulthood.

Habit reversal training for tics is another alternative. This involves becoming acutely aware of when you are about to have a specific tic and then performing an action that is incompatible with the tic. For example, someone with Tourette's might learn to press the side of the leg with the hand when feeling the urge to poke the eye, or to breathe deeply through the nose when the urge to shout arises. This intervention is called the competing response. . . .

Can Tics Be a Side Effect of Medications?

Bryan from NYC asks: I was on chemo when I was 16 and was given Thorazine for nausea. Sometimes, the Thorazine would make me feel as if I needed to move around—jerking my head, moving my arms and fingers, pacing, walking, etc. I could choose NOT to do those things, but it felt extremely uncomfortable (hard to resist an irresistible urge). I've always wondered if there was some similarity between my brain's reaction to the drug and what's happening with Tourette's.

Thank you for sharing your stories.

Dr. King and Dr. Leckman respond: Thorazine (chlorpromazine) and other so-called neuroleptic drugs can sometimes cause the acute onset of a variety of movements, including a very restless ants-in-the-pants feeling and behaviors like the ones you describe. The medical term for this is akisthisia, which comes from the Greek for "unable to sit."

Since the various neuroleptics are also sometimes *helpful* for tics and other symptoms of Tourette's, it's not surprising that they probably all affect some overlapping brain circuits and systems, especially in the area of the brain known as the basal ganglia, and hence produce similar sensations and urges. But the syndrome you are describing is distinct from ordinary tics and Tourette's.

One of the theories about Tourette's is that it arises from the failure to properly filter, or "gate," sensory and motor nervous system signals in the brain, so that un-bidden sensations make it into one's subjective conscious awareness. It is possible that the Thorazine might have contributed to a temporary failure of this filtering pro-cess in your case. However, in animal studies conducted more than a decade ago in San Diego, Neal Swerdlow and his colleagues found that Thorazine actually improved sensori-motor filtering or gating.

Alternatives to Drugs for Tourette's

Michael from Atlanta asks: I am 25 with Tourette's syn-drome. I take 15 mg of Abilify daily to reduce my tics, and it works great most of the time. However this is a very expensive medication and no other medication seems to work. I took myself off of Abilify for two weeks and my tics got worse. I was snorting violently to the point where my throat became inflamed. I am back on it now and the snorting is slowly dissipating.

I don't want to be on medication anymore, but I feel that I have to because my tics cause me to hurt myself. What are my options, if there are any other options, be-sides the experimental surgery?

Dr. King and Dr. Leckman respond: It is wonderful that the Abilify is helpful. Within a few years, it should be available as a generic compound and therefore much less expensive.

It's hard to know from your description of taking yourself off of the medication, but in general, it is im-portant not to discontinue anti-tic medication abruptly, because, even if such drugs do not seem to be fully effec-tive, stopping or reducing the dose suddenly can lead to a "rebound" flare-up. Such flare-ups can be avoided by a more gradual taper.

There are other experimental treatments for severe cases of Tourette's, including low frequency repetitive transcranial magnetic stimulation, or rTMS. In this pro-cedure, an electromagnet is positioned on the scalp over

Tourette syndrome is closely related to obsessive-compulsive disorder, which often manifests in excessive hand washing. Similar therapies are often used in the treatment of both disorders. (© John Greim/Photo Researchers, Inc.)

part of the brain called the supplementary motor area (SMA). Activating the magnet for brief periods sends pulses of magnetic waves into the brain, which may help to reduce tics, perhaps by altering rhythms in the brain.

There have been a series of case reports on rTMS, from Italy as well as from our group at Yale along with investigators at Columbia University.

We are currently conducting a research project to study the potential benefits of rTMS for Tourette's in a randomized placebo-controlled trial. The procedure typically involves 30 to 60 minutes a day of treatment for several weeks, but it is completely noninvasive.

CHAPTER 3

Living with Tourette Syndrome

The Anatomy of a Tic

Beth Krah

Beth Krah is a writer who has Tourette syndrome as well as obsessive-compulsive disorder and attention-deficit/hyperactivity disorder. In the following piece Krah describes an episode of tics in detail to help readers better understand what these symptoms are like. She compares the experience of tics to having millions of bubbles of energy multiplying inside her body, invading all of her senses. She is extremely sensitive to light, sound, movement, and temperature. She shakes, trembles, and feels compelled to hit herself. In response to various deep itches, she grimaces and contorts her face. Laughter, reading, and watching movies might help, but sleep provides little rest because she has anxious dreams.

If you are a parent, friend, or clinician of a child with Tourette Syndrome, I know that you ache watching the child going through difficult times with tics, and you feel desperately helpless. Your heart goes out, wanting

Photo on facing page. Tourette syndrome patients often must endure generalized anxiety and mood disorders. (© **acbag/ Alamy**)

to ease the child's discomfort, but you feel like an outsider, and are at a loss for what to do. I'm sure you would gladly trade places in an instant if you could. If only.

What's going on inside the child's mind? How can you help?

I'd like to attempt to describe a tic from the onset to give you more clarity and insight into what the experience is like. It is not my intention to offer options or recommendations for treatment, but rather to help enable you to understand the episodes when they do occur. Also, this is a personal account of what I have gone through, not necessarily what everyone experiences. Each individual is different.

Millions of Bubbles of Energy

My doctor once compared Tourette Syndrome, or more specifically, tics, to a Whac-A-Mole game at an amusement park. You hold the weapon in your hand, ready to strike at whatever pops up. By the time you whack at it, three more pop up. As soon as they disappear, the first one re-appears, sometimes with more force than before. It's frustrating, to say the least.

Imagine your entire body filled with millions of tiny bubbles filled with energy. Not unlike the Tasmanian Devil. Never resting, high octane bubbles, multiplying inside your body. That's what I feel like when I'm having a tough time. I feel restless. My breathing begins to accelerate. Things I try to focus on become fuzzy; not necessarily by sight, but in my mind. They're not as clear as before. I can't concentrate. Too much is happening inside. My neck feels weird. I feel this tiny rudder at the base of my skull that wants to turn my head back and forth, up and down . . . violently at times. (I've actually given myself whiplash because of this.) My big toe starts "thumping." All those tiny energy bubbles infiltrate my whole system. My eyes try to roll up and back into my head as far as possible. I begin to shake and tremble as I notice the heel of my hand aiming straight for my forehead again. I have to hit my forehead. I don't know why. I need to feel the pressure of something against my head.

My husband wants me to stop. He thinks I might injure myself. I once asked a doctor if that was possible. He said, "Yes, you could do brain damage." Oh. But I have to do it. I don't know how not to.

Excessive Sensitivity

Sometimes my husband has to pin me down and just hold me there until I can calm down. I have to fight him. I want desperately to wrestle with him, but he's afraid someone might get hurt. Most likely me. My sensory receptors seem highly over-sensitive to everything from light and sound to temperature and movement. My feet are hot, or cold. I can't get comfortable at all. The sun is too bright. Everything is too noisy. Too loud. Too cold. Too hot. Something may move and startle me. I just about jump out of my skin! My feet are really, really hot. So are the palms of my hands. I can't do anything to change this. It drives me nuts! My foot begins to shake or "flick." On my waterbed, I feel as stiff as a board. My husband says, "Just relax." Yeah, sure, okay, I can do that . . . not! I try to pretend this isn't happening . . . pretend I'm normal. Ha!

I tell myself, "Just stop all this. You're normal. Just stop and think of something else. Pretend you don't have Tourette's." That lasts a total of maybe three seconds. I hold my breath and stiffen myself as hard as I can. Maybe, just maybe, if I hold my breath long enough, I could faint. Then I'll be able to relax, right? Oh, to have something that could knock me out. Something that would calm me down, allow me to relax, let me sleep.

I can fully understand the desire to take something that will immediately put me to sleep. But what if I don't

> ## FAST FACT
>
> Research psychiatrist Barbara Coffey states that most adults with TS also have generalized anxiety and mood disorders.

wake up? I want to enjoy my life. I'm having too much fun enjoying life. I live life to the fullest! I don't want to stop that. There are too many things I want to learn how to do yet. I just want to stop the pain. Can life ever be that perfect this side of Heaven? I guess I'll just have to wait. Sometimes I don't feel like waiting a month for some of these medications to work. But I also don't want to screw up my poor brain any more than it is now.

My eyes start to itch. Everyone thinks I wear contacts. Okay, think that if you want. Maybe it's easier that way. But it's just another tic. Another mole to whack. To tell you the truth, they just itch . . . a lot! I blink a lot, try to rub them, put drops in them. Nothing seems to help. It seems to itch behind my eyes, behind my nose, my ears, and my face. I try to itch my ears. What a pain! Q-tips just don't hack it. It itches too deep in my head. So I end up making facial contortions and grimaces, thereby looking really silly, stupid, or just plain weird. How do you itch your brain? That's what it feels like.

Stuck, Dizzy, and Tired

Sometimes my brain feels funny. That's the only way I can describe it. It's almost like someone switched the wires around in my head. Like someone got in there and unhooked all the wires and put them in the wrong places. Go put 'em back! I don't like this feeling! I feel like I'm on hold. Like my brain went on "pause" and I'm stuck. I remember standing in front of my dresser, staring at it. The conversation with my brain went something like this: "Okay, get dressed." But how? "Just get dressed." But I don't know what to do! "Look, how many times in your 36 years have you done this?" A lot? "Okay, first open the drawer." How? What drawer? I'm stuck. I don't know what to do! Help!

That's about the time I begin to turn in circles. I keep going until I fall on the floor, or until my husband tries to stop me. I'm dizzy, confused, and tired. Please, please just let me sleep. Sleep seems to be the only escape. But sometimes, when I'm wired, all I can do is walk in circles around the house. I've measured the distance of some of these walks. I've covered more than a mile just walking through our kitchen, hallway, dining room, and back through the kitchen again.

Laughter and Music Help

Sometimes my five-year-old sees things that I'd prefer he not see. He gets this concerned look on his face. "Daddy, what's wrong with Mommy?" Most of the time I can turn the tic into something funny. Make a funny face or tickle him. Every night he prays that the "D's" (OCD [obsessive-compulsive disorder], ADHD [attention-deficit/hyperactivity disorder], Tourette Syndrome) would "stay far, far, far, far away from our whole family." Not that he understands what the D's represent, but he knows full well he doesn't want them anywhere near him.

Having Tourette syndrome has been compared to the Whac-a-Mole game. When one disorder is dealt with, three more may subsequently pop up. (© **RMUSA**/Alamy)

When I lay down for bed around midnight, I get as relaxed as I possibly can. But a board can only bend so much. I begin to tic again. Lately, I've been able to read for a few hours until I can't focus anymore. Then I may be able to fall asleep, usually around 2 A.M. Sometimes watching a movie may help. Sometimes I've gone up to the office to work on the budget, which just proves how desperate I am. The reading has to be something that I'm genuinely interested in, otherwise, forget it. Humor helps a lot. Whether it's a comic book or book of humorous stories, laughing seems to help get my mind off of myself. Sometimes I can browse through a magazine and get decorating ideas. Another thing that seems to help me calm down is music. For me, it's usually something like classical music, soft lullabies, or just listening to the birds sing.

Dream Battles

If I sleep well, I usually wake up feeling like a truck ran over me, totally exhausted. And if I need to get up, I'm not sure how I'm going to. All night long I've been battling things in my dreams. I'm so tired of getting shot, worrying about my son dying, and planning funerals. It just wears me out. Staring at the ceiling, I'm still somewhat in a daze. I have to lie there and try to sort through everything. What really happened? What was only a dream? Is my son asleep upstairs, or did he really die last week? It may take up to a half hour to go through everything and make sense of it all. Canceling out one dream at a time. I feel like someone's going to have to peel me off the bed like a fruit roll-up. I'm limp, totally exhausted, and have no energy whatsoever. But I can already feel Mr. Hyde's tiny energy bubbles lying deep beneath the surface like a restless tiger,

waiting . . .

biding his time . . .

to once again take over my life.

A Teen Struggles with Coprolalia and Bullying

Austin

The following selection originally appeared in *That Darn Tic,* a newsletter by and for youths who have Tourette syndrome (TS). The writer, Austin ("Carl" in the narrative), describes a challenging day in school when he was scolded and laughed at because he exhibited motor and vocal tics. On his way home he got in a fight after unintentionally uttering a racial epithet. His tics—along with his obsessive-compulsive disorder—seem to be a source of tension in his family—but watching a documentary about TS and playing the cello help him to feel more comfortable and confident. When he wrote this narrative, Austin was a sixteen-year-old student in Toluca Terrace, California.

I walked up to the door. There was a large piece of paper on it that read "Detention." I wanted to leave, but slowly I moved my hand to the door handle. I opened the door and walked straight to the back and sat down hoping the teacher wouldn't notice me back there. Unfortunately she did.

"Carl, come sit up here in the front."

I stood up and walked slowly to the front of the class, all of the other students were staring at me. My head started jerking uncontrollably as I walked up. My knees started bending. I bounced up and down. Before I reached the chair up front the last knee bend took me all the way down to the floor. My classmates were all laughing.

"Carl stop doing that. We have no need of a class clown."

Unable to Stop

On my knees, I started cussing uncontrollably.

"Carl! STOP!" she yelled, but I couldn't. It was like I was sneezing, I could hold it in, but it would still come out and even if I did hold it, it would come out even more vigorously.

I finally yelled a curse word and ran out of the class. This has happened every day for the past two weeks ever since I got off of winter break. The first sign of this was when I was sitting at a picnic table with my aching feet in ski boots next to a snowy mountain.

Now walking on the sidewalk on my way home I was counting every crack I saw. My head straight down and my mouth moving, I looked as if I were talking to myself. To add to that I was doing the knee bends.

More Trouble

I heard somebody say, "Hey look, there's the creep." I looked up and it was James, an African American boy that was a grade higher than me. I tried to get away, but he grabbed me by the arm. "Where you goin' buddy?" he said.

I then said the "n" word uncontrollably.

"What did you say?!" James asked.

I kept saying it and I couldn't stop. I closed my eyes trying to stop and suddenly I felt pain in my stomach. James had gotten me in a headlock and was punching me in the stomach over and over and over. I pulled him over my shoulder and on to the ground. A quick strike to the face and I was out of there.

My mom saw me walking towards the house and yelled, "Dinner!" When I saw her I felt loved. She was the only one who, even though she couldn't understand what was wrong with me, stood by me and never punished me. I sat down at the table as my mom gave me a plastic fork.

"Why don't you give him a metal fork?" my father said.

"He chews on them and it hurts his teeth," mom argued.

"You can't keep treating him like a child. He needs to grow up." They broke out into an argument. It ended with my dad going outside and taking a walk to cool down.

I took my food up to my room and sat on my bed feeling that every fight that my parents had was all my fault. I sat chewing on the plastic spoon trying to stop, but it was no use. As I ate I thought about what was wrong with me. To distract myself, I turned on the TV. A documentary called, "I Have Tourette's but Tourette's Doesn't Have Me" popped up.

It was about kids who had a condition called Tourette Syndrome. They had the same problems as me, just in different forms. "That's what I have!" I said to myself. I watched it for the next 30 minutes writing things down and I started to understand. It said that Tourette's is also paired with Obsessive Compulsive Disorder, which is why I always count the cracks on my way home.

> **FAST FACT**
>
> Among children with TS, 27 percent have moderate or severe forms of the condition, reports the Centers for Disease Control and Prevention.

Music Brings Relief

When the documentary was over I picked up my cello and started playing it for the first time in a month. It seemed that while I played all my problems just went away and I was comfortable. No cussing, counting or sudden head movements, just my cello and me. In the documentary there was something for every one of those kids that made them feel comfortable and in control. For me it was music.

That night I laid down in bed feeling able to get to sleep without any problems. My mother walked in and kissed me good night. I was ready for school, for teachers, for my problems, and for the next day. I felt as if I could answer any question about my condition.

It has been six months since then and everybody looks and talks to me as if there is nothing wrong with me.

I have Tourette's but Tourette's doesn't have me.

Seeking the Beauty of Stillness

Annette Racond

The author of the following essay, Annette Racond, has exhibited the symptoms of Tourette syndrome (TS) since the age of six but was not diagnosed until she was twenty-eight. She has been frequently disheartened over the years, living with a condition that is widely misunderstood and misrepresented in the media and taking medicines that provide minimal relief from her tics. However, hearing news about another TS patient whose symptoms were reduced by deep brain stimulation has given her hope that she might one day find true rest from her tics. Racond is a writer in New York City.

Certain moments in my life are like sharply focused snapshots that never fade. I was in my flannel pajamas watching TV in my parents' bedroom in Douglaston, N.Y., the day Neil Armstrong stepped onto the moon. More than a decade later, when news broke of John Lennon's death, I was cramming for a test in my dorm room at Boston University.

On April 1, 2004, I had another such moment: My mother called to tell me that Jeff Matovic, a 31-year-old husband and father from Lyndhurst, Ohio, had become the first person with Tourette's syndrome in the United States to be treated with deep brain stimulation. His doctors say the procedure has so far relieved Mr. Matovic of the tics that came with his disorder. He is no longer a constant prisoner to the abrupt and repetitive muscle movements and vocalizations that made his life unbearable. Mr. Matovic can now experience the beauty of stillness.

A Sense of Hope

As a fellow Tourette's syndrome sufferer, Mr. Matovic's story has given me hope that maybe I, too, can be freed from my tics, twitches, bobs, nods, grunts, squirms, hiccups and jolting motions. Even though I exhibited symptoms of Tourette's syndrome at age 6, the disorder was not diagnosed until I was 28.

Before that, numerous doctors had assured my parents and me that I would "outgrow" my tics. Over the years, I was told by members of the medical world to engage in more "daring" sex, to surround myself with plant life and to try "tribal therapy," removing my clothes and letting my inner child break out into a scream.

After an accurate diagnosis was finally made by doctors at New York-Presbyterian Medical Center, I was told there was no cure in sight. The best I could hope for was the minimal relief provided by drool-promoting drugs.

Misleading Information

Not only is it difficult to live with the symptoms of Tourette's syndrome, it is even more difficult to live with the stigma. Coprolalia, involuntary swearing and cursing that has its basis in neurobiology, is the main aspect of

The author was inspired by the story of Jeff Matovic (pictured), who was the first Tourette syndrome patient to have electronic devices implanted in his brain to control tremors.
(© AP Images/Tony Dejak)

Tourette's portrayed in the media. Yet just a small minority of people have coprolalia, and I am not among them.

Television shows like *Law and Order* present an unrealistic and frightful view of Tourette's. Because inaccurate information is so widespread, potential employers are often afraid I might shout obscenities at their clients, or at them.

Despite these obstacles, I have forged ahead. At 44, I have spent a good portion of my life learning to accept my circumstances and to discover what I can do. I can run. I can write. I can be funny. I can also learn: I earned a master's degree from New York University.

My family and friends supplied encouragement when I felt defeated. "They'll probably find a cure in the process of looking for something else," I was often told, but never really believed.

A Jaw-Dropping Moment

Witnessing a medical breakthrough of this magnitude in my lifetime was highly unlikely. Mr. Matovic urged his doctors at the University Hospitals of Cleveland to use a deep brain stimulation technique previously reserved in the United States for treating the shaking associated with Parkinson's disease. The procedure involves implanting electrodes into the part of the brain involved in controlling movements, then attaching these electrodes to a pacemaker using wires.

The results were evident sooner than anyone had anticipated, shocking even the doctors.

"This is what we refer to as a jaw-dropping moment," Mr. Matovic's neurologist, Dr. Brian Maddux, told *Good Morning America* on April 1 [2004]. Tourette's syndrome, a so-called orphan disease, had finally made international headlines.

Orphan diseases, commonly defined in the United States as conditions that affect fewer than 200,000 people, do not normally generate the same attention, or financing that more mainstream diseases do. Celebrities rarely speak on behalf of them. The real medical muscle is primarily focused elsewhere— on new techniques of cosmetic surgery, for example.

But while acquaintances of mine are getting the fat sucked out of their thighs and put into their lips, I can't

FAST FACT

According to the Tourette Syndrome Association, one out of one thousand people have TS.

escape the wrath of these relentless tics. Finally, someone took a chance to help one man overcome Tourette's syndrome, and I'm optimistic this will lead to many more recoveries.

My mother's phone call opened up the possibility of a new way of life for me, a life where I can be still in the still of the night. Some Americans thought the coverage of Neil Armstrong's walking on the moon was a hoax. Others did not believe that John Lennon was shot. Imagine their reactions if these events occurred on April Fool's Day.

But on that very day, I began believing in the power of medicine.

A Student Uses Humor to Teach About Tourette Syndrome

Holly Leber

In the following selection reporter Holly Leber profiles Rhett Sewell, an English major at the University of Tennessee who has Tourette syndrome. Diagnosed in the third grade, Sewell began giving speeches during his junior year in high school to raise awareness about the condition. Sewell recalls middle school as being his most difficult time, Leber notes, because the medications he was taking gave him anxiety and caused him to gain weight. So he decided to go off his medications and get involved in activities that he enjoyed: public speaking and acting. Sewell finds that his symptoms tend to decrease when he is acting or doing anything that requires concentration. He works as a counselor at Camp Twitch and Shout, a summer camp for children with TS, and plans to pursue acting or teaching as a career. Leber is a columnist for the *Chattanooga Times Free Press* in Tennessee.

SOURCE: Holly Leber, "UTC Student Uses Humor to Educate About Tourette Syndrome," *Chattanooga Times/Free Press,* December 10, 2010. All rights reserved. Reproduced by permission.

Sometimes, Rhett Sewell introduces himself as Rhett with Tourette.

"My name," the 20-year-old University of Tennessee at Chattanooga [UTC] freshman, said, "was a lovely stroke of irony. Why not use it in a positive sense?" According to the National Tourette Syndrome Association, the condition "is a neurological disorder . . . defined by multiple motor and vocal tics lasting more than one year." At times, Sewell blinks his eyes rapidly. Other times, he shakes his head or tosses it almost violently. Sometimes he'll make staccato noises or clear his throat. From time to time, he raises his arms above his head.

That hand-raising gesture he actually picked up from a friend. "For lack of a better word," he said, "you can 'adopt' somebody else's tics."

The same friend adopted his vocal tic. "Serves him right," Sewell quipped.

How It Happens

Tracy Colletti-Flynn, public relations manager for the Tourette Syndrome Association, says signs point to the disorder being related to dopamine, a brain chemical.

Sewell explained: "We are completely at whim to the signals we are getting from our brain." He said he can feel the tics coming on, but trying to control them is like trying to suppress a sneeze.

"I'm the one making the movements, I'm the one making the noises, and I'm doing that in response to the signals I'm getting from my brain," Sewell said. "My brain is constantly telling me 'make this noise, make this noise, make this noise.' And I'm the one who has to react to that."

Trying to hold back a tic, he said, is like trying to dam a river. Eventually the dam breaks. Trying not to tic too much, he said, can cause his chest to tighten and his breathing to become difficult.

Different environments affect his tics, and excitement or anxiety can make the tics more active. "If I'm focused on different things, my tics are a little bit less," he said.

Raising Awareness

Diagnosed in the third grade, Sewell started giving speeches to raise awareness about TS [Tourette syndrome] during his junior year of high school. Soon, he began to make regular appearances in schools around Georgia. Sewell's goal in 2011 is to begin giving talks in Tennessee. In October [2010], he spoke at UTC as part of the campus Disability Awareness Month. "One of the most impactful things he did was a motor-tic simulation," said Leslie Harms, assistant director of UTC Office for Students With Disabilities. "He had people writing down the Pledge of Allegiance while simulating motor tics. Every third word we wrote, we had to erase and rewrite it. Then when he gave a verbal command, we had to tap the edge of the desk." The activity, Harms said, helped her to understand the many brain signals Sewell has coming at him on a daily basis.

During presentations, students ask questions ranging from how TS affects his social interactions to how it influences his self-esteem. One of his most amusing questions, he said, always comes from ninth graders. "They always ask if I tic while I'm having sex." He doesn't. "Sleep and sex," he said, "that's always the two things you never have to worry about ticcing during." Being open about his condition has allowed Sewell to develop a strong sense of confidence and charisma. His social life, therefore, is not much different from most other college students. "I've got plenty of dates," he said. "I'll meet someone and of course one of the first conversations is always going to be Tourette Syndrome, because it's there. After that I'm not 'that guy I met with Tourette's,' I'm just Rhett; and we go out and things like that. And you, know, you've always got to have that twitchy kid at the party."

Media Misconception

One of the strongest misconceptions about Tourette Syndrome is that coprolalia—the involuntary use of obscene and/or socially inappropriate words or phrases—is a typical symptom. In fact, only about 10 percent of people with TS have coprolalia or copropraxia, which means making obscene gestures. "It's a very, very rare symptom," said Colletti-Flynn, "but that's what the media likes to portray, because they think it's funny." The TSA issued a press release following a 2007 episode of the television cartoon series *South Park*, which featured a character with strongly copralalic TS. Despite concerns, however, the group conceded that the portrayal was not entirely misleading. Sewell said he wants to dispel misconceptions, but he doesn't condemn the media portrayal of TS. "Even me, with Tourette's Syndrome, I laughed at (the *South Park* episode), but those are just tools for humor devices." He likes to incorporate humor into his presentations, he said. When the inevitable question of what his condition prevents him from being able to do [arises], he responds, tongue-in-cheek: "Well, I'll never be able to be a librarian and I'll always lose at the quiet game. So I'm heartbroken about that."

FAST FACT

Two relatively uncommon Tourette tics are echolalia, repeating the words and movements of others; and palilalia, repeating one's own words and movements.

Coming to Terms

It wasn't always easy to laugh about Tourette Syndrome. "Middle school is bad for anybody," he said, "but when you throw the Tourette Syndrome in the mix, it makes it a whole new adventure." Because the exact cause and genetic structure of TS is not yet known, said Colletti-Flynn, there is no medication specifically for the illness. Some patients are given pills designed for other conditions, however the negatives often outweigh the positives. When he was prescribed blood-pressure medication and anti-depressants, Sewell rapidly gained weight and became anxious and jittery. "I went through middle school being the fat, awkward, twitchy kid," he said. "I shut down." Eventually he told his parents he had to go off the meds because they were doing more harm than the Tourette Syndrome. "Going into high school, I looked back at what had happened and I realized I had wasted my middle school career sitting at the bottom of the wall at my own pity party," he said. So he started learning as much as he could and eventually began public speaking. He rebuilt friendships, became involved in National Honor Society, and found a new love: acting.

Acting gives Sewell respite from Tourette Syndrome. When he's on stage, he said, the symptoms lessen because he's able to be the character. "It's really easy for me to push those tics back, but as soon as the curtain drops, it's right back up again." He hopes to pursue acting professionally, but the English major is also considering teaching. Having TS can present challenges in an academic environment, though Sewell, who has a moderate case, said his college experience is not much different from his peers. He is eligible to register with the Office for Students with Disabilities for extended test time and separate testing locations, but he chooses not to, "mainly because I'm stubborn." "For me taking tests actually really helps because I'm so focused," he said. "My tics kind of go out the window for a little while." There are good days and bad days. "There are certain times you wouldn't know I had Tourette, usually if I have a lot of things going on. Other days, it's everything I can do to keep my head above water." Sometimes he has to leave a class or social event so he can collect himself and get the tics under control. It's frustrating, especially for a college student, when a bad tic day interrupts his life. "I've got stuff I've got to go do," he said. "I've got people to hang out with. I have things to study for. I have assignments. I've got to go talk to girls." Having Tourette Syndrome, Sewell said, has shaped who he is: a self-described average 20-year-old kid.

"And to a ridiculous degree I'm a nerd," he added. "I'm a 20-year-old guy with a box of Legos in his college dorm room."

Camp Twitch and Shout

Each summer, Sewell spends a week as a counselor at a camp for children with Tourette Syndrome: Camp Twitch and Shout.

"I love the name," he said, laughing. "It's great." Twitch and Shout is operated by the Tourette Information Center & Support (T.I.C.S.) of Georgia, a research and support non-profit based in Smyrna, Ga. The camp is in Winder, Ga.

The severity of the condition varies among the campers, all of whom have Tourette Syndrome, and the counselors, only some of whom do. Such an environment, Sewell said, can actually aggravate, his condition. "When you see someone with Tourette Syndrome, it makes you hyper aware of your own Tourette Syndrome, so our tics got a lot worse. I was ticcing like crazy trying to help these campers out, they were ticcing like crazy." Though the goal is to give young people a sense of belonging and confidence, Twitch and Shout is a camp, he emphasized, not a group therapy session. "It's everything you would think a camp would do, we just pay a little more attention because the kids have Tourette," he said. And what might start out as being more noticeably a camp for kids with TS, "by the end of the week, it's just kids at camp. It's like 'You're twitchy, I'm twitchy, let's go do canoes.'"

Tourette Syndrome as a Fuel for Musical Creativity

Independent on Sunday

The following piece originally appeared in the *Independent on Sunday*, a London, England, newspaper. It is a profile of Nick Van Bloss, a British piano virtuoso with Tourette syndrome (TS). Van Bloss's tics—violent head shaking, eye rolling, and self-punching—emerged suddenly at the age of seven. During his childhood in the 1970s, TS was not well understood; physicians often diagnosed him as "attention seeking" and prescribed powerful drugs for his condition. At age eleven he discovered that playing the piano made his tics disappear. Gifted with the ability to memorize music quickly, Van Bloss studied piano at the Royal College of Music—but after suddenly losing the ability to play during a competition, he abandoned the instrument for more than a decade. Eventually, Van Bloss fully accepted his TS condition and found that he could use it to fuel his creativity.

Neurologically speaking, Peter Shaffer's *Amadeus* has a lot to answer for. It was largely thanks to this jeu d'esprit [witty composition] on genius that people started thinking Mozart suffered from Tourette's syndrome (TS). He didn't, of course, but the connection between music and Tourette's is sometimes very real—and never more so than in the case of the pianist Nick Van Bloss, who is defying his condition in the most dramatic way. Yet "defy" is the wrong word: the 38,400 tics he endures daily may once have pushed him out of concert life, but he's now discovered how to harness them, to a point where their rhythms have become—at least in part—the key to his singular artistry.

The man who arrives for interview is physically graceful and wittily urbane, and during our conversation there is not a tic in sight. This, he says, is because he is suppressing them, as he does when on stage. Once back in the privacy of his car he will apparently yelp, bark, blink, nod, and clench his jaws so violently that his teeth will be in danger of breaking. He will also repeatedly open and close the door as he drives along, since obsessive-compulsive disorder [OCD] is a side-symptom. Friends prefer not to accept his offer of a lift on motorways, he says with a laugh.

I first became aware of Van Bloss thanks to a *Horizon* [a British TV program] documentary entitled "Mad But Glad," in which he explained to a fascinated Oliver Sacks how his music dovetailed with his Tourette's; he then dazzled Sacks with a virtuoso performance. This film had been triggered by the publication of Van Bloss's very moving autobiography, *Busy Body*, and it led in turn to his being invited to make a series of recordings for Nimbus. The first of these, of [Johann Sebastian] Bach's *Goldberg Variations*, was released to critical acclaim in February [2011]; the second—of Bach's keyboard concertos, with Van Bloss leading from the keyboard—is due out soon.

"A Shaking Freak"

So, the story. Born in 1967, he was, he says, a normal, happy, clever boy growing up in a bohemian Islington [a London neighborhood] family. One morning when he was seven, he woke up and couldn't stop shaking his head violently. "It happened overnight: I was suddenly a shaking freak, and there was no explanation. I was told to stop it, but all I knew was that my body was making me do it." His parents quickly understood this and were supportive, and his schoolmates accepted it: extreme classroom cruelty—from teachers as well as pupils—would only come later. Initially, his main suffering was physical—all the muscles in his neck hurt from the shaking, and he'd be in pain from rolling his eyes so hard in their sockets: "It was like a fictional possession. I was self-harming, constantly punching myself. I realised later that a lot of people who were burnt at the stake in the Middle Ages would simply have had this affliction."

> **FAST FACT**
>
> Neurologist Oliver Sacks maintains that many people with both TS and OCD experience heightened sensitivity, which can enhance creative abilities.

Van Bloss's childhood was made infinitely harder by the fact that, in the Seventies, Tourette's was barely on the medical radar. Ignore him—even smack him—was the first medical advice his parents got: "attention-seeking" was the usual diagnosis, and heavy doses of Valium were prescribed which, since he couldn't swallow them, he routinely hid behind the fridge. But when he was 11, a miracle occurred: he fell in love with the piano. Touching things was always one of his Tourette's-induced compulsions, and when he put his fingers on the keys his tics disappeared, their rhythms becoming subsumed into the music. Moreover, his preternatural ability to retain numbers and physical details—another remarkable TS side-effect—allowed him to memorise music perfectly, without even trying. As school became a living hell where he was routinely kicked, punched, and reviled, the piano became his haven.

A Dark Time

He was accepted into the junior section of the Royal College of Music, and in due course the senior section welcomed him with open arms. He was a star student, and found himself making friendships; he discovered quite happily that he was gay, and his TS-induced conviction that he was an ugly freak began to dissipate; he seemed on the verge of a successful performing career. But then, in the finale of a piano competition in Spain which he'd been tipped to win, he suddenly froze with his arms in mid-air: under stress, Tourette's had finally conquered him.

This was the beginning of a 15-year period in which he contracted cancer, abandoned all thought of being a pianist, got rid of his piano, and survived with financial support from his family. "I was not playing physically, but I was still playing inside all the time," he explains. Finally, on an impulse, he acquired a new instrument, but when it arrived he couldn't summon the courage to touch it. "I covered it with a tablecloth to try to block it out of my mind, because I didn't want to go near this thing which had broken my heart. It represented to me all that should have been, and could have been, but wasn't. I was in a dark time, and it ate away at me." Meanwhile, his Tourette's was behaving in what seemed an increasingly predatory way. The metaphor he constantly uses to describe it is one of greed: he felt he had to feed it like a monster, answer its insatiable demands.

One day a thought occurred: accept it. And when he did, everything changed. "In truth," he concluded at the end of his book, "I'm a happy Tourettist. I'm not half a person courtesy of Tourette's syndrome. I think I'm larger than life. And that suits me just fine." That was five years ago, when he still assumed a concert career was out of the question. His professional re-entry has proved as extraordinary as everything else in his zig-zag story.

Harnessing Tourette's

His next step was to harness his enemy, realising that it could work for him. "Tourette's is my fuel," he says now. "It's the fire within, the burning energy. And the ironic, even beautiful thing about my condition is that once I sit down to the piano, there's nothing to see." Invited to make a recording, he learned Bach's *Goldberg Variations* in a mere three weeks, mostly not even at the piano: "I had it in my mind for many years, even though I hadn't played it. It had always seemed to me too big, too monumental to touch. There's an incredible amount of joy and humour in it, and I had fun with it." The super-sensitive touch which Tourette's had forced him to cultivate was now deployed on every note of every piece he played: his brilliant technique was natural, inbuilt. The recording itself, which needed very few retakes, had that almost preternatural clarity which now characterises all his playing. He then took the plunge and gave a concert: "As I

Music therapy has helped many Tourette syndrome patients find relief and boost their creativity. (© Erich Schlegal/Corbis)

looked out at the Steinway [piano] on stage, it felt like a homecoming, and I felt at peace." He got rave reviews, but then found himself deluged with offers of a sort he felt compelled to refuse.

"I didn't want to be told to play [music by Russian composer Pyotr Ilich] Tchaikovsky, then to abuse the audience, then to gyrate wildly as I go offstage—which was what some potential backers wanted. That sort of vulgar celebrity, as in [the 1996 film] *Shine*, might bring in a beautiful crowd, but not the crowd I want. For me, musical integrity is paramount. I don't want to be labelled 'the Tourette's pianist.'"

What he wants with his forthcoming series of Bach CDs is validation from the profession: "That people should say, quite simply, this is good, and he's serious." He should relax, because it is, and he is.

GLOSSARY

**attention-deficit/
hyperactivity
disorder (ADHD)**
A neurobiological condition characterized by hyperactivity, impulsivity, distractibility, and an inability to sustain attention. Frequently a co-occurring disorder in patients with Tourette syndrome.

basal ganglia
Masses of gray matter in the cerebral hemispheres of the brain that are involved in the regulation of voluntary movement. Tourette syndrome has been linked to these areas of the brain.

biofeedback
A method of learning to modify a body function, such as blood pressure or muscle tension, with the help of an electronic instrument.

CAT scan (CT scan)
Computerized axial tomography, a series of computerized X-rays of the brain that show detailed brain structure. (Also called computed tomography, or CT, scan.)

**central nervous
system (CNS)**
The brain along with the spinal cord.

chronic
Long lasting or recurring often.

clonidine
Originally a drug used to treat high blood pressure, it is sometimes used to control tics and ADHD symptoms.

cognitive dulling
A potential side effect of neuroleptic drugs; may involve short-term memory loss and slowed thinking.

comorbid conditions
Term used to describe medical conditions that occur with each other; however, there is no direct causal relationship between the conditions.

**comprehensive
behavioral
intervention for tics
(CBIT)**
A form of behavioral intervention that incorporates habit-reversal training, which teaches a Tourette syndrome patient to channel the urge to tic into a less noticeable behavior.

compulsion	A powerful urge to do or say something—usually something irrational or contrary to one's will.
coprolalia	The involuntary uttering of obscene words, seen in a minority of Tourette syndrome patients.
deep brain stimulation (DBS)	A treatment for movement disorders in which electrical pulses are sent through wires that have been surgically implanted into the brain.
degenerative	Progressively worsening.
***Diagnostic and Statistical Manual of Mental Disorders* (DSM)**	A manual published by the American Psychiatric Association that includes diagnostic criteria and systematic descriptions of various mental disorders.
dopamine	A neurotransmitter involved in the control of movement. Tics may result from the abnormal functioning of this transmitter.
dyslexia	Difficulty in reading, spelling, and writing words.
echolalia	The involuntary repetition of a word or phrase just spoken by another person.
echopraxia	The involuntary mimicking of others' gestures and movements.
movement disorders	A group of neurological conditions that cause abnormal voluntary or involuntary movements or slow, reduced movements. Huntington's disease, Parkinson's disease, restless legs syndrome, and Tourette syndrome are all movement disorders.
neuroleptics	A class of drugs (including aripiprazole, haloperidol, and pimozide) that suppress spontaneous movements.
neurotransmitters	Any of several chemical substances that transmit nerve impulses across the small gaps between nerve cells.
norepinephrine	One of the brain's neurotransmitters involved in the function and formation of dopamine and serotonin.

obsessive-compulsive disorder (OCD)	A condition in which people become trapped in a pattern of repeated, unwanted thoughts (obsessions), and a pattern of repetitive behaviors (compulsions). Frequently a co-occurring condition with Tourette syndrome.
palilalia	The involuntary repetition of one's own words or phrases.
premonitory urges	Sensations experienced by some Tourette syndrome patients prior to a tic.
remission	The absence of symptoms of a chronic disorder for a period of months or years.
serotonin	A brain chemical associated with emotions, particularly feelings of well-being.
tardive dyskinesia	Uncontrollable movements of the mouth, tongue, and lips. Can occur as a side effect of neuroleptic drugs prescribed for Tourette syndrome.
tic	An involuntary, sudden, spasmodic movement (motor tic) or involuntary vocalization (vocal/phonic tic).
tic disorder	A condition characterized by the presence of tics.
Tourette syndrome (TS)	A tic disorder and movement disorder characterized by the chronic presence of both motor and vocal/phonic tics.
transient	Brief, or producing effects for a short period of time.
trigger	Something that brings about a disease or condition.
waxing and waning	A naturally occurring increase and decrease in the severity and frequency of TS symptoms.

CHRONOLOGY

1489   The first account of what would later be known as Tourette syndrome (TS) appears in *Malleus Maleficarum*, a book by Jakob Sprenger and Heinrich Kramer. The account was a description of a priest—presumed to be possessed by the devil—suffering from tics.

1709–1784   English poet, essayist, and lexicographer Samuel Johnson displays signs of TS, including phonic tics and involuntary movements.

1756–1791   Austrian composer Wolfgang Amadeus Mozart suffers from hyperactivity, mood swings, and tics. Later, in the twentieth century, some experts speculate that he had TS.

1825   French neurologist Jean-Marc Gaspard Itard describes the symptoms of a noblewoman, the Marquise de Dampierre, who suffers from motor tics, echolalia, and coprolalia. Itard notes that the marquise would try harder to suppress her most obscene utterances.

1857   Georges Albert Édouard Brutus Gilles de la Tourette is born.

1882   French clinician and neuropathologist Jean-Martin Charcot establishes a clinic at the Salpetriere Hospital in Paris. He assigns his student-resident, Gilles de la Tourette, to study patients with tic disorders.

1885   Gilles de la Tourette publishes *Study of a Nervous Afflic-tion*, an account of nine patients, including the now-elderly Marquise de Dampierre. He concludes that the vocal tics and involuntary movements spring from a specific syndrome.

early 1900s   Most experts believe that TS is the result of brain lesions or psychogenic disorders. Patients with tics are generally thought to be suffering from unresolved psychological disturbances.

1920–1960s   Psychoanalysis is the preferred treatment for TS.

1961   French physician Jean N. Seignot publishes a paper on treating TS with the drug haloperidol.

1965   American psychiatrist Arthur K. Shapiro, known as the father of modern tic disorder research, treats a TS patient with haloperidol.

1968   Psychiatry professors Arthur K. Shapiro and Elaine Shapiro publish an article that strongly criticizes the psychoanalytic approaches to treating TS. They argue that TS is a neurological, rather than a psychological, disorder.

1972   The Tourette Syndrome Association (TSA) is founded.

1972–1973   The National Institutes of Health turns down a grant proposal from the TSA, believing that there are no more than 100 cases of TS in the United States and only 485 cases worldwide.

mid–1970s   Articles about TS in *Good Housekeeping*, the *New York Times*, and the Ann Landers advice column generate a response that proves that there are many undiagnosed cases of Tourette's in the United States.

1981 The American television medical drama *Quincy, M.E.* airs an episode devoted to TS.

2000 The American Psychiatric Association publishes the fourth edition and text revision of the *Diagnostic and Statistical Manual of Mental Disorders* (DSM-IV-TR). It revises the previous DSM-IV, maintaining that symptoms of tic disorders do not necessarily impair function or cause distress.

2004 In a radio interview with Terry Gross, Canadian comedian Dan Aykroyd explains that he had mild TS that was successfully treated with therapy when he was a preteen; a British made-for-television movie, *Dirty Filthy Love*, tells the story of Mark Furness, who has both TS and obsessive-compulsive disorder; Jeff Matovic is the first TS patient in the United States to be treated with deep brain stimulation.

2006 HBO produces the Emmy Award–winning documentary film *I Have Tourette's but Tourette's Doesn't Have Me*; Pete Bennett, a singer with TS, is featured in the British television reality show *Big Brother*.

2009 Nick Van Bloss, a British classical pianist with TS, returns to the stage after a fifteen-year hiatus.

2011 Aspiring musician Ruth Ojadi relates her struggle with TS in a British television documentary, *Tourette's: I Swear I Can Sing*.

ORGANIZATIONS TO CONTACT

The editors have compiled the following list of organizations concerned with the issues debated in this book. The descriptions are derived from materials provided by the organizations. All have publications or information available for interested readers. The list was compiled on the date of publication of the present volume; the information provided here may change. Be aware that many organizations take several weeks or longer to respond to inquiries, so allow as much time as possible.

American Academy of Child and Adolescent Psychiatry (AACAP)
3615 Wisconsin Ave. NW, Washington, DC 20016-3007
(202) 966-7300
fax: (202) 966-2891
e-mail: communications@aacap.org
website: www.aacap.org

Established in 1953, the AACAP is a nonprofit organization composed of over seventy-five hundred child and adolescent psychiatrists and other interested physicians. Recognizing that up to 12 million American youth suffer from mental, behavioral, or developmental disorders, the AACAP is dedicated to improving the quality of life for children, adolescents, and families affected by these disorders. Its website features a searchable database and links to "Facts for Families" articles on Tourette syndrome (TS) and its associated disorders, including "Tic Disorders," "Children Who Can't Pay Attention: Attention Deficit Hyperactivity Disorder," and "Obsessive-Compulsive Disorder in Children and Adolescents."

American Academy of Neurology (AAN)
1080 Montreal Ave., St. Paul, MN 55116
(800) 879-1960
fax: (651) 695-2791
website: www.aan.com

Established in 1948, the AAN is an international professional association of more than twenty-one thousand neurologists and neuroscience professionals who care for patients with neurological disorders. The academy publishes the *Neurology Journal* and the biweekly newsletter *Neurology Today*. Its website offers a searchable archive of disorders and patient guidelines, including "Tourette Syndrome" and "Botulinum Neurotoxin for the Treatment of Movement Disorders."

Centers for Disease Control and Prevention (CDC)
1600 Clifton Rd.,
Atlanta, GA 30333
(800) 232-4636
(888) 232-6348
e-mail: cdcinfo@cdc
.gov
website: www.cdc.gov

A branch of the US Department of Health and Human Services, the CDC serves as the national focus for developing and applying disease prevention and control, environmental health, and health promotion and education activities designed to improve the health of people in the United States. An A–Z index as well as fact sheets on TS, attention-deficit/hyperactivity disorder, and bullying are all available through its website.

Jaylens Challenge Foundation
PO Box 93653,
Lakeland, FL 33804
website: www.
JaylensChallenge.org

Jaylens Challenge is a foundation and a website that seeks to raise awareness about TS and its related conditions and to counteract bullying against the disabled. Created by TS patient Jaylen Arnold when he was nine years old, the site features fact sheets about TS, a blog by Jaylen, several videos, links to anti-bullying resources, and a chat forum.

Movement Disorder Society (MDS)
555 E. Wells St., Ste.
1100, Milwaukee, WI
53202-3823
(414) 276-2145
fax: (414) 276-3349
e-mail: info@move
mentdisorders.org
website: www.move
mentdisorders.org

MDS is an international professional society invested in the research and care of people with movement disorders, including Parkinson's disease, Huntington's disease, restless legs syndrome, and TS. It publishes the monthly *Movement Disorders* journal; *MDS News*, a monthly e-bulletin; and *Moving Along*, a tri-quarterly newsletter. The website's searchable database provides links to articles such as "Tics and Tourette Syndrome," "The Management of Tics," and "Update on DBS for Tourette Syndrome."

National Institute of Mental Health (NIMH)
6001 Executive Blvd., Rm. 8184, MSC 9663, Bethesda, MD 20892-9663
(301) 443-4513
(866) 615-6464
fax: (301) 443-4279
e-mail: nimhinfo@nih.gov
website: www.nimh.nih.gov/index.shtml

The NIMH is the US government agency that seeks to improve the treatment and prevention of mental illness through research in neuroscience, behavioral science, and genetics. The website includes a "Health Topics" page with links to extensive information on obsessive-compulsive disorder and attention-deficit/hyperactivity disorder, conditions that are sometimes seen in people with TS.

National Institute of Neurological Disorders and Stroke (NINDS)
PO Box 5801, Bethesda, MD 20824
(800) 352-9424
(301) 496-5751
website: www.ninds.nih.gov

A branch of the US National Institutes of Health, the NINDS conducts, fosters, and guides research on the causes, prevention, diagnosis, and treatment of neurological disorders and stroke. It also provides grants-in-aid to public and private institutions and individuals in fields related to its areas of interest. Included at the NINDS website are an index of neurological disorders and a TS information page.

Tourette Syndrome Association (TSA)
42-40 Bell Blvd., Bayside, NY 11361
(718) 224-2999
fax: (718) 279-9596
website: www.tsa-usa.org

Founded in 1972, the national TSA is a nonprofit and advocacy organization dedicated to finding the cause, cure, and effective treatments for TS. The TSA funds research, offers resources and referrals to help patients and their families cope with the problems associated with TS, and works to educate the public and dispel stereotypes and misinformation about the disorder. It publishes the quarterly newsletter *Inside TSA*; *That Darn Tic*, a newsletter by and for children; and an online young adult newsletter, *It's Not Just for Kids Anymore*.

Tourette Syndrome "Plus"
Leslie E. Packer
940 Lincoln Place,
North Bellmore, NY
11710-1016
(516) 785-2653
e-mail: admin@tourette
syndrome.net
website: www.tourette
syndrome.net

Tourette Syndrome "Plus" is a website created by Leslie E. Packer, a New York State licensed psychologist who specializes in TS and its associated conditions. The site offers numerous articles and essays on TS, attention-deficit/hyperactivity disorder, obsessive-compulsive disorder, sleep disorders, and other related conditions. Sample articles include "Tic- Related School Problems," "Bullying Among Children and Youth with Disabilities and Special Needs," and "Is Behavior Modification Appropriate?"

We Move
5731 Mosholu Ave.,
Bronx, NY 10471
e-mail: wemove@
wemove.org
website: www.wemove
.org

We Move is a nonprofit and advocacy organization that aims to improve awareness, diagnosis, and management of neurologic movement disorders among people living with these conditions and the professionals who care for them. Its website features a searchable directory of clinics and doctors who diagnose and treat movement disorders such as Parkinson's disease, tardive dyskinesia, and TS, among others. Also available at the site are links to articles and overviews on tic disorders and TS.

FOR FURTHER READING

Books

Ruth Bjorklund, *Health Alert: Tourette Syndrome*. Salt Lake City, UT: Benchmark, 2009.

Sandra Buffolano, *Coping with Tourette Syndrome: A Workbook for Kids with Tic Disorders*. Oakland, CA: Instant Help, 2008.

Susan Conners, *The Tourette Syndrome and OCD Checklist: A Practical Reference for Parents and Teachers*. Hoboken, NJ: Jossey-Bass, 2011.

Jeffrey Koterba, *Inklings: A Memoir*. New York: Houghton Mifflin Harcourt, 2009.

Howard Kushner, *A Cursing Brain? The Histories of Tourette Syndrome*. Cambridge, MA: Harvard University Press, 2000.

M. Foster Olive, *Psychological Disorders: Tourette Syndrome*. New York: Chelsea House, 2009.

James Patterson, Hal Friedman, and Cory Friedman, *Against Medical Advice: One Family's Struggle with an Agonizing Medical Mystery*. New York: Little, Brown, 2008.

Dylan Peters, *Tic Talk: Living with Tourette Syndrome: A 9-Year-Old Boy's Story in His Own Words*. Chandler, AZ: Little Five Star, 2009.

Mary Robertson and Andrea Cavanna, eds., *Facts: Tourette Syndrome*. New York: Oxford University Press, 2008.

Sheila J. Rogers, *Natural Treatments for Tics and Tourette's: A Patient and Family Guide*. Berkeley, CA: North Atlantic, 2008.

Douglas W. Woods, John C. Piacentini, Susanna W. Chang et al., *Managing Tourette Syndrome: A Behavioral Intervention for Children and Adults; Therapist Guide*. New York: Oxford University Press, 2008.

Sheila Wyborny, *Diseases and Disorders: Tourette Syndrome*. Farmington Hills, MI: Lucent, 2010.

PERSPECTIVES ON DISEASES AND DISORDERS

Periodicals and Internet Sources

Allison Brantley, "'I Tried to Stop': Fifteen-Year-Old Kayley Fights to Reclaim Her Life While Battling Tourette's," *Wilson (NC) Daily Times*, June 5, 2010.

Arian Campo-Flores and Catharine Skipp, "Taking on Tourette's: A New Approach to Stopping Tics Before They Happen Offers Hope to Thousands with This Disorder," *Newsweek*, September 3, 2007.

Centers for Disease Control and Prevention, "Tourette Syndrome: Treatments," March 5, 2012. www.cdc.gov/ncbddd/tourette/treatments.html.

Caroline Davies, "Comeback for Pianist Who Beat Tourette's," *Observer* (London), April 12, 2009.

Susan Jeffrey, "Children with Tourette's Syndrome and Chronic Tic Disorders Respond to Behavioral Therapy," Medscape Today, May 24, 2010. www.medscape.org/viewarticle/722270.

Roger M. Kurlan, "Approaches to Treating Tourette's Syndrome," *Physician's Weekly*, July 26, 2011.

Alison Lee, "Tourette's Syndrome," *Psychology Review*, April 2007.

Colleen B. Litof, "Understanding Tourette Syndrome and Providing Relief," *Applied Neurology*, August 1, 2007.

Mary Brophy Marcus, "A Boy's Battle with Tourette's," *USA Today*, October 20, 2008.

Jodi O'Donnell-Ames, "Most Teens Aim for Popularity . . . Others Just Hope for Simple Acceptance," *EP Magazine*, March 2009.

Christina Ottery, "Treating Tourette Syndrome with Deep Brain Surgery," Dana Foundation, March 29, 2011. www.dana.org/news/features/detail.aspx?id=31548.

Leslie E. Packer, "Treatment of Tourette's Syndrome," Tourette Syndrome "Plus," March 2011. www.tourettesyndrome.net/disorders/tourette%E2%80%99s-syndrome/treatment-of-tourettes-syndrome.

Steven Reinberg, "Tourette Syndrome Diagnosed in 3 in Every 1,000 Kids," *Consumer Health News*, June 4, 2009.

Tammie Smith, "Teen Strives to Educate Others About Tourette's Syndrome," *Richmond (VA) Times-Dispatch*, April 18, 2009.

Daniel Stimson, "Abnormalities in Brain Histamine May Be Key Factor in Tourette Syndrome," National Institute of Neurological Disorders and Stroke, September 14, 2010. www.ninds.nih.gov/news_and_events/news_articles/Abnormalities%20in%20Brain%20Histamine%20may%20be%20Key%20Factor%20in%20Tourette%20Syndrome.htm.

Tourette Syndrome Association, "Bullying 101: What Children, Parents, and Teachers Need to Know," *Inside TSA*, Spring 2010.

Mark Wheeler, "Behavior Therapy Effective in Reducing Tics in Children with Tourette Syndrome, Study Finds," UCLA Newsroom, May 18, 2010. http://newsroom.ucla.edu/portal/ucla/behavior-therapy-is-effective-158553.aspx?link_page_rss=158553.

INDEX